Anita Bell is best known as Australi... ...
mum. She lives with her husb... ...
menagerie of pets and farm a... ...
property in the Brisbane Valley. ... ...
aged 26 and has spent the last ... ...and
multitude of hobbies, including ... ...g, home
handicrafts and helping others to ...eir dreams of
financial independence. She is also a p...ular children's author
and spends much of her spare time encouraging students in
primary and high schools into new methods of creative
thinking, writing and finance.

YOUR KIDS' MONEY

HOW TO EARN IT, SAVE IT AND SET THEM UP FOR LIFE

ANITA BELL

RANDOM HOUSE AUSTRALIA

Random House Australia Pty Ltd
20 Alfred Street, Milsons Point, NSW 2061
http://www.randomhouse.com.au

Sydney   New York   Toronto
London   Auckland   Johannesburg

First published by Random House Australia 2005

National Library of Australia
Cataloguing-in-Publication Entry

Bell, Anita, 1967–.
Your kids' money.

ISBN 1 74051 368 1.

1. Money-making projects for children. 2. Children's allowances. 3. Finance,
Personal. I. Title.

332.024

Cover design by Darian Causby/Highway 51 Design Works
Typeset in by Midland Typesetters, Maryborough, Victoria
Printed and bound by Griffin Press, Netley, South Australia

10 9 8 7 6 5 4 3 2 1

Acknowledgements

A special thank you to Katherene McNeil for sharing the fun of writing puzzle stories with me. What fun we have trying to trick each other!

Sincerest thanks also Jenny Stubbs, Carolyn Keighley and Josephine Griffiths for their endless devotion to innovative learning opportunities, and to *The Learning Place*, a Queensland State Library initiative, for providing Internet chat rooms to help reach more schools than could ever by possible in person.

Thanks also to Meredith Curnow, Jessica Dettmann and the fabulous team at Random House Australia, without whom this book would still be a manuscript in cyberspace.

If you had a coin for every dirty nappy,
Would you invest them in the child,
Or spend them to be happy?

Contents

Important Note   **xi**

**1. An Introduction for Parents, Teachers and
   Guardians**   **1**
   On the subject of ASIC's discussion paper on
   financial literacy in schools   4
   Passing information on to your kids   5

2. Tools for Starting Early   **13**
   Financial theories vs. practical solutions   13
   Money trees   17
   On the subject of affording money trees   18
   On the subject of catching up   18
   Investment Strategy 1   19
   Investment Strategy 2   21
   On the subject of managed funds   25
   On the subject of risk   25
   On the subject of high, low and medium returns   26
   Investment Strategy 3   29

3. Financial Planning for the Unborn   **32**
   Advance budgeting for babies   32
   Top tips for baby budgeting before pregnancy   36
   On the subject of stockpiling   40
   Planning for childcare and/or viable alternatives   41

4. Government Cash After Birth   **43**
   Centrelink payments from birth to job searching   43
   Tax rebates and offsets   49

5. The Toddling Years – from Birth to Pre-pre-school   **50**
  Surviving maternity/parental leave   50
  Surviving day-to-day costs   51
  Pre-pocket money and non-cash rewards   53
  First cash concepts   54
  Progressing to pocket money   54
6. Planning Education Costs and Savings from Kindy to Uni   **60**
  On the subject of planning ahead for education
  costs   60
  Scholarships, bursaries and fellowships   63
  Annual tertiary education costs   68
  How will I afford it?   69
7. Primary Schoolers   **74**
  Lessons for cash handling and shopping for
  value   74
  Pocket money strategies for earning, spending and
  saving   75
  Strategy 1: Pocket money paydays   77
  Strategy 2: All-expenses-paid (plus optional bonuses)   81
  Strategy 3: Compromise with a flat allowance
  plus bonuses   85
  On the subject of paying bonuses to children   85
  On the subject of cash in lieu of presents   86
  On the subject of cash in lieu of parties   87
  On the subject of dollar-for-dollar deals   89
  Chores without rewards   89
  How much pocket money?   92
  Quasi-pay packets for volunteer work   96
  On the subject of borrowing money back from
  your kids   97
8. High School and the Teen Years   **98**
  Hobby jobs   99
  First taxes for children   102
  On the subject of tax and the age kids can work   103

Jobs for senior high school students   104
Other opportunities to make money   107
On the subject of dropping out of school early   109
On the subject of mentors   109
On the subject of making 'it' happen   110
9. Standing on Your Own Financial Feet   113
Assets from scratch   113
Inheritances   113
On the subject of mobile phones   114
On the subject of lending money or belongings
to friends   115
Starting to stand on your own feet   115
Credit rating   117
Avoiding mistakes that can set you back a decade   117
On the subject of honesty, finance and business   119
A finance quiz   119
10. Advanced Industry-level Literacy for
Teenagers   134
Topic 1: Types of industry   134
Topic 2: Types of work   134
Topic 3: Types of employee   138
Topic 4: Terms relating to pay   139
Topic 5: Types of leave   143
Topic 6: Terminology for interviews, awards
and industrial negotiations   146
11. The Sweet 16 – Extra Support Skills to Add
Booster Rockets to Your Teenager's
Financial Future   149
1. Prioritising with/without the fun-factor   150
2. Honouring family, work ethics and beliefs 151
3. Jargon interpretation   151
4. Goal setting   153
5. Career planning   154
6. Contingency planning (change management)   155
7. Rage management   156
8. Customer service   157

9. Cash handling and checking change 158
10. Pride, initiative and willingness in your work 158
11. Networking 159
12. Negotiating and bartering 161
13. Surviving workplace personalities 163
14. Asserting your rights as a consumer 163
15. Respect for laws and obligations to the Tax Office 165
16. Dress rehearsals 167
Bonus skill: Creative thinking 168

12. The GAP Years – Young Adults aged 18 to 21 170
Working holidays 170
Volunteer holidays 171
Lifestyle issues – Booze, entertainment and hobbies 172
On the subject of hobbies and business paperwork 173
Car insurance and betting against yourself 176

13. Investment Options, Banking and Packaging 178
Credit cards 178
Savings accounts 180
Term deposits and high-interest savings accounts 181
Overdrafts 181
Stockmarket shares 182
Investment property 188
Investment packaging 189
Superannuation 189
Family trusts 193

**14. Other Programs, Initiatives, Resources and
Opportunities 194**

15. The Game Zone 199
Coin games 199
On the subject of computerised finance games 202
Puzzle stories 202
Feeding dreams with fractured finance tales 206

16. A Happy Ending 220
Appendix I. Hints for Student Challenges 221
Appendix II. 50 Fun Rules for Success 227

IMPORTANT NOTE

Anita Bell is not and has never been employed in the finance or real estate industries. Her books are based on personal experiences in the hope of helping others enjoy the shortcuts – and avoid the traps – that she found in the process of retiring by age 26 and, with her husband, Jim, paying off four properties by the age of 29.

Anita does not provide one-on-one financial advice or make professional recommendations for any company, product or service. She does not charge fees for any of her financial guest-speaking events. And while some companies, products or services are occasionally mentioned in the interests of providing working examples, she does not receive or accept payment from any of the companies or lenders involved.

About *Your Kids' Money*

This book is the seventh in the series and is written primarily for adults and mature teens as an aid to improving financial literacy for the whole family. It also:

- provides unique, fun and practical activities for parents, teachers and students;
- serves as a useful supplement to curriculum units for financial literacy;
- provides alternative perspectives, based on experience.

Additional note for teachers

This book provides a wide range of resource material as suggested by the ASIC National Discussion Paper for Financial Literacy in Schools, based on the author's own experiences and successful seminars with students of various age groups.

1

An Introduction for Parents, Teachers and Guardians

Firstly, a big wave and hello to the fans of the *Your Mortgage* series who have not only enjoyed my fast, fun and adaptable shortcuts to financial success over the last six years, but who have also contacted me to ask if I can provide a book specifically aimed at helping with their children.

So here it is! And no ordinary book about finances for offspring either, since it contains a great deal of personal experience, unusual tips and shortcuts that also help you avoid the most dangerous pitfalls on the path to financial literacy and proficiency for the whole family.

In the chapters to follow, you'll find tools to help you consider the financial futures of your children, as well as tools and resources to help you teach them good habits, skills and attitudes from birth to young adulthood. In fact, I'm already grinning, knowing how many mature children and teenagers have taken over the financial reins for their families after reading *Your Money: Starting Out and Starting Over*, which was written for adults and teen-life *after* graduation. The cheeky tigers! Fancy learning so well and so early that they're able to teach their parents a thing or two! It's always exciting to see how resourceful and energetic teens can be when armed with both knowledge and opportunity.

This book aims to make it even easier. Think of it as a prequel to *Your Money: Starting Out and Starting Over* – packed with fun, easy to understand examples, role-playing challenges and discussion topics that parents, children and teens can learn together in order to make it through birth and childhood into the teen years and the transition years from school or uni into the workforce.

BEFORE WE BEGIN

It's important to understand my unique perspective in writing the series.

I purchased my first long-term asset as a 10-year-old, using pocket money earned through my own backyard hobby-business selling horse manure, homemade craft (sketches and knitting) and coaching younger children in English, maths and horse riding. I bought my first block of land when I was 16, and I'd paid off four properties completely by the time I was 29 – one of them while single and the next three in partnership with my husband, Jim. And that's while earning only low to modest wages and *without* needing to sell or 'release equity' from any property in order to purchase the next! Which, for those of you who don't yet understand the property market, is safer but slightly harder than the method used by most investors, who use equity and capital growth in one property to help fund the purchase of the next.

The process of achieving freedom from debt while earning only modest wages taught me, and later my husband, a truckload of unique methods for making every dollar count, with budgets, bank accounts, sanity allowances and shopaholic tendencies.

Did you know?

Yes, it IS still possible for your child to pay off their first home in five years without handouts from you (or save up to $250,000 on their first property) . . .
BUT ONLY if they start with a clean slate and have the basics of this book firmly in their grasp.

NOTES FOR PARENTS

Details and opportunities can change quickly in the world of finance, and it may seem like a daunting task to many parents who have lots to learn themselves before they're able to pass anything on to their kids. But I do hope you'll soon see how interesting, financially rewarding and fun it can be, especially by the time you reach the last chapters of this book and begin to group-learn as a family!

There are also a wide range of practical strategies provided for you with foundations in good old-fashioned hard work and honesty. And yes, there are even a few of my favourite alternative viewpoints which may help if some of the most popular financial theories fail for your family, because my own experience in achieving debt freedom by age 23 and retirement by 26 has taught me:

- No financial strategy will work for 100% of the people 100% of the time.
- There are no expensive secrets that you need to pay for. Nearly everything you need to know is available free from your local library, bank, building society or credit union.
- Following the flock in financial matters often results in a fleecing.
- The only person who can design a fully-flexible, reliable and portable financial strategy that perfectly suits your own situation, or that of your family, is YOU. Because you and your children are the only ones who can comprehensively compare quantitative values (things that can be measured or touched, like value for money, tax effectiveness and cost) with qualitative values (intangible and immeasurable things that are just as important, like 'enjoyability', convenience and suitability to future goals). The rest of us can only show you what's possible in order to help you learn adaptability, cynicism and determination – the three keys to fast-tracking your child's success *safely*.

Did you know?

Boxes of information suitable for sharing with student-aged children are highlighted by a drop-shadow like this.

Also unique to this book are the practical activities and 'bedtime stories' designed to help you share tips with your own children or students, which I've developed and field-tested with parents, teachers and students of all ages from schools, colleges and universities around the country.

ON THE SUBJECT OF ASIC'S DISCUSSION PAPER ON FINANCIAL LITERACY IN SCHOOLS

It's been a passion of mine for almost a decade to help plug the holes in the financial education for our children and target their needs before they're old enough to get into financial trouble. Then, early in 2003, the Australian Securities and Investment Commission (ASIC) – in their role as consumer guardians – commissioned a report on where and how financial education was being taught in Australian high schools. Co-funded by the Financial Planners' Association, this report was intended to help provide the framework for establishing a national strategic direction for consumer financial literacy in Australia, following extensive anecdotal feedback and figures suggesting that financial illiteracy was beginning to cost the country billions per decade as well as having significant socio-economic repercussions on Aussie families.

Published in June 2003, the 100-page report and discussion paper invited feedback from the community and industry professionals. (See also Chapter 14: Other Programs, Initiatives, Resources and Opportunities.) Over the next six months, the federal government and the 15 members of the consumer and financial literacy taskforce (drawn from volunteers from a wide range of interested corporate, community and government sectors) established the first Financial Literacy Foundation, with a budget commitment totalling $26 million over the five financial years from 2004–05 to 2008–09, in order to:

- co-ordinate and improve financial education initiatives and projects among public, private and community organisations;
- work with state and territory governments to improve school

curricula by the addition or improvement of financial literacy subjects with extra support and training for teachers;
- establish a website to provide an information hub for financial literacy education and information resources.

For more information on the taskforce phone 1800 020 008, or see their website: www.cfltaskforce.treasury.gov.au.

PASSING INFORMATION ON TO YOUR KIDS

Our options for earning income and managing expenditure changed so much over the last few decades that many of our own parents weren't able to pass on their financial knowledge and skill-base to us. It took them a lifetime to learn, and now we've a got a situation with practically three generations all trying to play catch-up. So please try not to feel any embarrassment about having holes in your own financial literacy, and accept the very high probability that you'll be learning new things from your kids as they progress through each of the puzzles and student challenges. Try not to be frightened or intimidated by it, as too many parents seem to be. It's my hope that sharing the thrill of adventure and discovery with your children and teenagers will help to re-charge your own aspirations for financial vitality.

In short . . . HAVE FUN!

That's an order.

WHY BOTHER?

I've heard it whispered many times: *Why bother educating ourselves in order to pass financial skills on to our children, when they'll pick everything up for themselves eventually, just as we had to?*

So for those of you who've been thinking along these lines, I'd encourage you to ask yourself three questions:
1. If you could stop your children falling prey to financial scams and mistakes that risk destroying their lives, would you?
2. If you could do it in a way that helped you as well as your children, why wouldn't you?

3. With average personal debts skyrocketing from $1601 per adult in 1996 to $5162 in 2004 (and that's not counting an average of at least $100,000 for the mortgage on the family home), have you really picked things up as well as you think?

> **Money is a tool for developing character and life skills.**

If you think that financial education should be left to the school system, then perhaps you should think again on that topic, too.

Why? Because the process of becoming financially literate is a lifelong enterprise that starts long before children enter school, multiplies in proportion to experiences gained outside a school environment and continues well after graduation day into adulthood and even into retirement.

So no matter how much effort is poured into formal methods of financial education in schools, we – as parents and guardians – are the only people in a position to provide constancy and consistency to the learning curve for our children as well as support outside of the school environment using live budgets and meaningful financial decisions. (See also Chapter 11: The Sweet 16 – Extra Support Skills to Add Booster Rockets . . .)

Still not convinced? Then consider the costs and risks to society generally. Every year Australians lose over $200 million to financial mistakes and scams, due mainly to gullibility, lack of consumer information and financial illiteracy.

National surveys into financial literacy in Australia[1] suggest a gloomy outlook for school leavers, reporting that 18- to 24-year-olds are the consumer group most likely to suffer the lowest levels of financial literacy – that's the first six years out of high school, when it's most needed!

---

1 Surveys commissioned by the ANZ Bank.

Additional research commissioned by ASIC[2] in association with their 2003 Discussion Paper for Financial Literacy in Schools also discovered there were:

- no formal courses of study in financial literacy in Australia;
- no formal or systematic approach to teaching financial literacy, even in those subjects that cover commercial or business studies;
- limited opportunities for the teaching of financial literacy;
- extremely limited resources for the teaching of financial literacy, with up-to-date Australian texts for teachers virtually non-existent.

Since then, extensive programs and opportunities have become available (see Chapter 14 for details), but the populace has fallen into two major categories: the horses who may be led to water but are too content to drink, and the ones who realise how thirsty they've been and plunge straight in. You must take action now, or you and your children will be left behind while the rest of us continue to race ahead.

ON THE SUBJECT OF GIVING CASH VS. GIVING KNOWLEDGE

Obviously many parents would want to give their children both cash and knowledge if they could afford it, while others have very strong desires one way or the other. But it's a decision you'll have to make for each child independently, considering their individual talents and tendencies to either work or be lazy. For example, it's very hard to avoid the urge of wanting to help an honest, hardworking and appreciative child as much as you can, but it's probably wise to hold back on the same urge where a lazy, unappreciative child is concerned to avoid worsening the situation by rewarding negative attitudes.

With luck, patience and perseverance, you should be able to pass on skills and knowledge at the same time as together

---

2 Erebus Consulting Partners commissioned by ASIC for the Financial Literacy discussion paper.

you build an investment portfolio using the tips from this and later chapters. I've also provided the following story (one of my favourite ancient parables) to provide you with an interesting extra point of view, which in some respects is as relevant to modern children as it was to young men over 3000 years ago.

THE OLD MERCHANT AND THE TWO BAGS OF WEALTH
A rich old merchant had two sons who both wanted to take over the family business. So he gave each of them a bag of wealth and sent them out into the world with instructions to use the contents to grow wealthier and prove which of them was the most worthy.

The first bag bulged with gold and the first son took it and ran out into the world to make his start. The second bag appeared to be empty and the second child begged his father to know why his brother had been granted such a great advantage. But the rich old merchant consoled his son that he loved both children equally and explained how the bag had already taught its first lesson of business: to seek understanding in the process of filling it. Then he spent the next week sharing lessons of his experience in business and bade farewell to his son, who hurried off, keen to catch up on the head start afforded to his brother by the bag of gold.

At the end of the year, the first child returned as a beggar with his clothes tattered, his feet bare and his face ravaged by the stress of hunger and weather.

'What have you to show for the bag of gold?' asked his father, but the beggar-son fell to his knees and wept.

'You didn't give me enough,' he replied. 'I started well, spending the first half to set myself up with a fine house and many camels, but then I lost everything to poor investments, bad clients and disreputable money lenders.'

Then the second child rode in at the head of a long camel train with his empty bag now full of gold and each beast labouring under the weight of more gold, treasure and gemstones. So the first child ran to his brother and begged to know what had been inside the second bag, and the younger man emptied the gold into his father's lap as a gift, then tossed the empty bag to his brother.

Extra moral to use if reading this story to children
Never drool over the advantages that others seem to have, just do the best you can with whatever you can gather.

THE GENERATION LAP VS. INFORMATION OVERLOAD
Parents have been shaking their heads at the differences between themselves and their children for . . . well, generations! But the traditional concept of a generation 'gap' is fast becoming a generation 'lap' as our kids and/or grandchildren overtake us in the information they have at their fingertips.

But while processing skills, especially using the Internet, are one key element that sets us apart at times, the differences between adults and kids are rarely as radical as you may think. A mature child or teenager faces many of the same dilemmas as do adults in making their own sound financial decisions and consumer choices based on research, value, cost and effort involved in saving up in advance – even if you don't agree as a parent on the 'value' of the item they're choosing. And the solutions are equally obscured behind the common barriers of poor consumer advice or information overload.

So when commencing the learning process afresh together, both adults and children will benefit the most if they're able to recognise the skills of each member of the family when it comes to having the experience and ability to process information quickly.

ENGAGING THE RELUCTANT LEARNER
Obviously, every child is an individual, so it's unreasonable to expect the same learning strategies to work for all of them. The following suggestions have been adapted from the time-honoured business principles of Dale Carnegie's bestseller *How*

to Win Friends and Influence People to help engage or re-engage a student's interest in financial literacy strategies.

1. Criticism of someone who is learning a new concept will always boomerang back, because the student switches to defence mode instead of staying open to new ideas. So avoid criticism, condemnation and complaints wherever possible when teaching financial principles to your children.

2. Reward correct decisions or financial behaviour (especially the small achievements, in the case of a beginner) by giving

---

Did you know?

Your local supermarket provides a perfect co-learning ground amidst 'information overload', especially for children aged five to nine, at a place where the generation gap is the narrowest (since we all eat food). Encouraging children to choose a new or favourite product from the extensive range, while comparing prices for value, provides opportunities for children to gain valuable financial decision-making skills. Asking older children to help you hunt for the best value biscuits, drinks and cold goods not only helps to keep their hands and minds busy, it also allows you to introduce the concepts of value by weight or volume.

Likewise, the generation lap can be put to good use by encouraging older, Internet-savvy children to assist in hunting for prices, value, features and warranty details each time your family is in the market for electrical goods, furniture, landscaping requirements or cars.

Handy hint: using your children as 'human calculators' to keep track of the running total of your groceries also provides excellent practice at putting school maths to practical use. For children aged five to seven, try rounding each item to the nearest dollar before helping them add to the total, while for older children, rounding to the nearest fifty cents is easily handled.

> A financial concept is easier to remember if it feels like your own idea.

honest, sincere appreciation wherever it's warranted. At the same time, keep a wary eye open to help discourage bad habits from forming. This fundamental principle, by the way, is used for training everything from dogs, horses and laboratory rats to sportsmen, executives and TV personalities.

3. Don't force ANY finance ideas down your kids' throats. Much better to back off if you experience problems and let them discover ideas for themselves by:
   a. putting them in positions where they need to handle cash or make purchasing decisions as regularly as possible;
   b. leaving book-marked books or open newspapers with useful information lying around where they're likely to find them.

4. When trying to motivate children to learn, don't think about what *you* want. Think about what *they* want and help them get it by offering them opportunities and options.

5. Be prepared to relinquish power or delegate whenever possible. For safety, you have to be careful what decisions you allow them to make and how far down the wrong path you'll let them go before they get into trouble. But if you can stand the nerves, let them set off in the wrong direction for a while before they discover for themselves that your experience would have saved them – a very hard thing for anyone to admit.

6. Be cheery and keenly interested in sharing great new financial tips with your family, and when your children come to you with new ideas, return their excitement. Treat the negative experiences as learning opportunities.

FIXING YOUR OWN FINANCES AT THE SAME TIME AS TEACHING YOUR KIDS

It's important to remember why tighter control over your own expenses will affect your kids' money through their assets, cash-flow and investment ratios for the first 15 to 20 years of their lives (at least!):

1. You can't invest in your child or provide initial cash-flow through pocket-money or cash-for-chores if you barely have enough to scratch yourself.
2. Kids learn by example, so if your own money skills suck, there's a big chance your munchkins will suffer the dreaded loop of history too unless you do something about it.
3. Clearing existing debts as much as possible and/or building a fat safety-net in extra mortgage repayments *before* you pack bags for a romantic weekend away will very often make the difference in your ability to borrow, upgrade or even renovate during those first five years of your child's life.
4. Statistically, financial worries provide one of the main reasons why co-parenting adults fight through to divorce. Anecdotally, financial worries make a baby's cry sound many times louder than it is.

So now, having learned why we have to grab a firm hold over the reins of financial literacy for ourselves, as well as for our children, and having dispelled the worst of the negativity and excuses, it's time to move on to the tools you need to maximise your effectiveness: by starting early.

2

Tools for Starting Early

It's common knowledge that the best and cheapest way to afford anything is to plan ahead for it. And so it is for our most precious life achievements: children. Yet most couples seem to leave their preparations to the last minute or, at best, only a few months prior to conception. This chapter aims to provide the information and tools you need to understand the true value of starting early with your savings and financial planning for each child, as well as understand the financial consequences of failing to prepare your own finances up to two years in advance. The repercussions on your entire family can last a lifetime.

> Some people plan a month's holiday up to a year in advance, but neglect financial planning for children until the last few months prior to conception or birth. Where's the logic in that?

FINANCIAL THEORIES VS. PRACTICAL SOLUTIONS

Let's start our discussion for and against planning early with the oldest theory: that wealth grows tallest over a lifetime when planted the soonest. It's a concept that pre-dates the invention of the drachma in Athens with its 65 to 67 grains of fine silver in the late 7th century BC.

It's also a theory upon which all modern managed funds, superannuation policies and long-term investments for our children are based because of its fundamental and rather obvious truth. But it's a theory that can be challenged under more recent conditions where families have to juggle mortgages, tight budgets, low rates of return on savings accounts, high management fees and fluctuating levels of income. It's difficult to justify saving (for anything, not only for your children) into an investment that earns 3% interest (or less!) while you're still struggling to pay off a mortgage with interest rates of 7% or more – especially now that extra mortgage repayments can no longer be considered as 'gone forever' (because they can be re-drawn or borrowed against whenever you need or desire them). For some people, the process of saving small amounts of money into a savings account regularly is not only boring and slow-to-reward, it's also a drag on family budgets that are stretched to the max. For others – especially those who are striving toward early debt freedom (i.e. in 10 years or less) – it can be far more rewarding financially to make every cent work as hard as it can to pay off personal debts *before* you start saving (at a faster rate) in time for your children to enter high school.

It's vital to understand the time-proven (and potentially mind-blowing) benefits of planning secure financial futures for our children as soon as possible (often on their behalf before they're even born!), against the costs of raising children under modern circumstances and the opportunities made possible by financial products which have only recently come into existence. But before we get to the specific details and basic maths that will help you develop your own plan, it's helpful to get a wider understanding of the principals of saving, opportunities and alternative possibilities.

DESIGNING OPPORTUNITIES WITH MODERN FINANCIAL STRATEGIES AND PRODUCTS

One of the biggest problems facing financially illiterate families is their lack of understanding of the options available for saving/investing/spending. For example, any family could tell you how they'd spend a million dollars if they won it, but when it comes to making the small dollars work the hardest on a weekly basis, they often miss some of their best opportunities.

Before we discuss the three main financial strategies that can help fix this situation, let's consider the following table, which gives a snapshot of some of my favourite ways for putting an extra $100 to hard work:

Options for spare $100 found through better budgeting	Long-term impact
1. As an extra repayment off a $200,000 loan at 8% that you're taking the full 30 years to eliminate.	Save $998 in interest payments.
2. As an extra repayment off your store card/credit account when paying off $1000 to $3000, assuming it stays pretty well maxed out over the first 1 to 8 years of your child's life.	Save $240 to $255 in interest payments.
3. As an extra repayment off your car or other personal loan.	Save $160 in interest payments.
4. Investing in a high-interest-earning savings account (which nearly always earns between 1% and 6% LESS than what you're being charged on your mortgage).	Earns only $17 to $75 interest.

So it becomes obvious that making extra repayments can be far more valuable than investing.

Handy hint: Mortgage interest and purchasing expenses for your own home are not tax deductible, so the examples here only compare like with like by assuming that your credit cards, store credit, car loans and overdrafts are not used to purchase anything that is fully/partially tax-deductible.

Such financial products can often be used to buy things that are fully/partially tax-deductible provided they are used for the purposes of earning an income. But you must keep records as evidence of purchase and work out – possibly with the help of your accountant – what percentage of the things you buy are used in whole/ part by your family business or by yourself or your children to generate taxable income. For example, credit cards can be used to pay phone bills or interest on overdrafts used to buy stockmarket shares.

EXCUSES EVAPORATED
Over the last decade, the main reasons parents have given me for not starting to save or invest (either for themselves or for their children) have been:

1. No incentive – 'Returns are low, taxes are high and it's more immediately rewarding to buy luxuries or pay the cash off our mortgage instead.'
2. Poor budgeting skills – 'We can hardly afford to pay living expenses as it is!'
3. Forgetfulness – 'Oh, yeah, I've been meaning to do that . . .'
4. Naïveté – 'Why didn't I think of that?' often followed by 'How?'
5. Bad experience – 'Been there, burned out, bought the T-shirt.'
6. Fear – 'There's no guarantee of return.'
7. Resentment – 'Fund managers are living the high life on my money while I'm slaving to make contributions.'
8. Apathy – 'I'm doing okay, and nobody ever gave *me* a financial kick-start.'

The first point, as I've shown, is extremely valid provided the purchase of luxuries is balanced with careful debt management. As for extra mortgage repayments, if it's financially possible for you to clear the debt on your own home in five to 10 years without either you or your partner falling pregnant in the first four years, then you will almost certainly open gaping financial opportunities for both you and your children in both the medium and long terms. (Short term from the perspective

of this book and *Your Mortgage* being three years or less,
term being three to five years. Financial advisors
consider three to 10 years as medium term, but I've always
trouble thinking of my life in more than three- to five-year
blocks at a time.)

Points 2 to 7 are relatively easy to beat or re-program for
success by using some of the skills you need to achieve the first
point, like budgeting skills, caution, investigation skills, patience
and a dash of self-discipline.

The last point, however, can be highly controversial because
it boils down to the fundamental differences in parenting style:
**When sending your child out into the world, is it
better to hand them a bag of cash or encourage them
to learn how to earn cash for themselves?**

MONEY TREES

We all wish we had one. As income-earning adults with growing superannuation policies, we practically do. But how many
of us are prepared to plant a small financial 'seed' and nurture
it, pay after pay, for our children? Answer: not many. Because
we all feel the pain of locking extra voluntary contributions
into our superannuation policies or education funds year after
year, at the same time as growth is consistently set back by the
annual blight of tax and management fees. It's not much of an
incentive to save for either ourselves or our children.

But what if you could dodge hefty management fees, achieve
ever-increasing growth and pluck the fruits of your money tree
as each goal-stage of growth was achieved, with the added flexibility of being able to chop your tree down and spend it all
during an emergency without the added penalty of nasty withdrawal fees? Well, you can. It's called investing (using a range
of products to suit the small investor). And although there's
not much we can do about the tax conditions in this country
for small investors and parents who are saving and investing
on behalf of their children, there's quite a lot we can do about
making our money trees grow as fast as – or even faster than –

they would if they were locked into much less flexible savings funds.

However, before we get to the basic maths and juicy details of how and where to plant money trees, we need to put every family on the same playing field by discussing affordability and the possibilities for catching up.

ON THE SUBJECT OF AFFORDING MONEY TREES

Regular contributions can nearly always be afforded much more easily after your mortgage and debts are streamlined and working properly, even if you're still a few years away from achieving debt freedom. Many families have reported finding $40 to $240 per month that had previously been slipping through their fingers! Other families have simply bitten the bullet and diverted small automatic payments out of their weekly/fortnightly income into a do-not-touch savings account, and then learned how to live without it.

Once you've decided to set up your automatic contributions, it usually only takes a month or two to get used to your new budget for living expenses. (See page 70, Finding savings in a strangled budget.) If you're still finding it financially painful to stash away contributions for your money tree after two months, then double-check your budget for savings elsewhere. Alternatively you could cut back on the amount you're trying to stash away until you can afford to increase it again later, even if you have to do it with a lump sum from a tax refund, back-pay or other minor windfall.

ON THE SUBJECT OF CATCHING UP

In my opinion, planting a money tree – regardless of whether it grows from a small seed at birth or a bigger lump-sum before your child enters high school – is worthwhile, since you don't have to give the money to the child as a gift 'when the time comes' at ages 16, 18, 21 or upon marriage or leaving home. You could choose to:

a. Spend the money on things that benefit you directly as well as the child indirectly, like buying an investment property in your own name that's close to your child's job or university so they can live-in and manage your tenants in exchange for free or super-cheap rent.
b. Offer your teenager the chance to earn the money tree after another decade or so by:
   • giving them the chance to take over contributions as soon as they graduate from high school (regardless of whether they have a job or earn jobsearch allowance) and there-fore proving themselves worthy through evidence of good saving habits;
   • sharing costs of contributions dollar-for-dollar as soon as your teenager is able to earn an income, and then sharing the proceeds in another decade or two.

LETTING BASIC MATHS REVEAL YOUR MAJOR OPTIONS FOR GROWING MONEY TREES

I've included a 'bedtime story' version of the following invest-ment strategies on page 206 to help you share the basic concept with your primary school aged children, but for mature students and adults, the mathematics can easily speak for itself:

INVESTMENT STRATEGY 1: The slow, methodical and conservative option

If you start with an opening balance of $100 (perhaps from your Centrelink Maternity Payment, see page 45), then save $20 per fortnight (from your paypacket or fortnightly family payments which are paid per child for the first 16 years) into a high-interest-earning, no-fee savings account or term deposit, which is earning an average of 7% interest per year and com-pounds (pays interest back into the account) at least twice a year, then you can expect returns of at least those shown in the following table:

Projected savings assuming an opening balance of $100, regular payments of $20/fortnight and 7% income from interest per year which is reinvested:

Years involved	Contributions so far* $	Interest earned* $	Total accumulated $
8	4200	1500	5700
10	5300	2400	7700
16	8400	7200	15,600
18	9400	9600	19,100
21	11,000	14,200	25,200
30	15,700	38,200	53,900
40	20,900	88,900	109,800
50	26,100	199,600	225,700
60	31,300	428,600	459,900
*Rounded to the nearest $100			

I've used 7% calculations for these long-term averages for savings accounts, even though we've just come through a long period of returns averaging only 3% to 5%, because historically over the last 30 years 7% is a much more likely long-term average and market indicators for rising interest rates suggest we should be earning better returns on our term and savings accounts again soon.

Note how your interest earnings pass a 'pivot point' in the 18th year (when the interest rate is 7%) where the earnings from interest begin breeding at a faster rate than your contributions each year. Unfortunately for most parents, the 18th year is also when they've usually been taught to cash out in order to help pay for university fees – *before* they realise that the benefits of their many years of efforts are only just beginning.

BUT ... for the last decade or so, pathetic returns on savings accounts (in the order of 0.5% to 3%) have made it unlikely for most parents to see the benefits of long-term savings. At the same time, those parents who *did* begin to diligently stash cash away back in the eighties (when term accounts paid a much healthier 8% to 15%) would have been silly to leave it sitting around in cash accounts after the returns crashed and opportunities opened up in the sharemarket and investment properties instead.

So if the last two decades of extreme fluctuations in returns have taught us anything, it's to look at the pivot points for each saving strategy and shift cash around more often than the fund managers would perhaps like us to. (Be extremely careful to avoid accounts or funds that charge ugly exit fees which attempt to keep us trapped.)

Did you know?

The following pivot points are handy to remember when comparing interest rates for various long-term investments. Use them to help understand the true cost of chopping down your money tree early to pay for education expenses or to buy a car for your child, when the investment may be in the transition stages of becoming a real money-spinner.

4% per year is 31 years

5% per year is 25 years

6% per year is 21 years

7% per year is 18 years

8% per year is 16 years

9% per year is 14 years

10% per year is 12.5 years

INVESTMENT STRATEGY 2: The slightly faster, often fluctuating but still relatively conservative option

Using the same kick-start of $100 plus fortnightly contributions of $20 as described in the example above, but investing it this time into slightly less conventional but more profitable financial products (like shares), which either grow steadily or

grow-shrink-grow-shrink-grow-shrink almost annually on a
cycle that averages a steady growth of about 12% a year, you
can expect returns as shown in the following table:

**Projected savings assuming an opening balance of
$100, regular payments of $20/fortnight and 12%
income from EITHER interest per year which is reinvested OR growth in capital (underlying) value, or a
combination of the two:**

Years involved	Contributions so far* $	Interest earned* $	Total accumulated $
8	4200	3000	7200
10	5300	5000	10,300
16	8400	17,400	25,800
18	9400	24,500	33,900
21	11,000	39,400	50,400
30	15,700	140,900	156,600
40	20,900	443,800	464,700
50	26,100	1,473,800	1,499,900
60	31,300	4,798,700	4,820,000
*Rounded to the nearest $100			

Twelve per cent! Are you crazy?

Not where potential returns over multiple decades are
concerned. We've just been through a relatively long period of
very low interest rates and consumer memories are notoriously
short, so I can understand if you don't remember the 10% to
14% government bonds, term deposits or high interest savings
accounts of the late 1980s and early 1990s (at a time when
mortgage interest rates were soaring between 14% and 17%!).

In the last decade skyrocketing property values meant that in
effect, the sharemarket was broadly advertised as being the
least productive option for investment returns, and by compar-

ison to property, it certainly was. But to illustrate how 12% is feasible, the table on the next page shows a few examples of blue-chip shares which were all purchased using the 10 easy steps from the last chapter of *Your Money: Starting Out and Starting Over.* (See also page 27 for details of ASIC's recommendations on acceptable rates of return from investments.)

Handy hint: The price samples are averaged assuming that shares are held continuously for the entire period through bear markets – where prices are clawed down by market conditions – as well as charging bull runs when prices race away. But returns can be maximised by taking advantage of the seasonal fluctuations throughout the year in order to buy and sell (usually only one or two times a year for conservative investors) to increase returns by an extra 10% to 40% per share. It just depends on how much paperwork, time, stress and share trans-actions you wish to manage.

Please also remember that blue-chip shares are the 'plodders' of the sharemarket – relatively slow but usually reliable – while many 'green-chip' companies (strong and fairly reliable growth companies) earned up to double these returns during the same period, (provided you didn't hang onto them each time they slid back too far towards their purchase price).

I hope this table also illustrates how direct investment into the ordinary shares of these popular 'blue-chip' companies has provided a very reasonable and rather 'conservative' return which averages well over 12% per year.

Did you know?
In the sharemarket, money that bounces regularly from one place to another is called 'hot money'. So in long-term investments, most conservative investors aim for 'lukewarm to simmer'.

Sample share performances of companies purchased using the 10-Step method from Chapter 13 over the last decade:

Share (alphabetically)	Purchase $price each @ date	'Current' $price each @ 2/6/05	Average growth % per year•	Typical dividend returns per year*	Approx. return per year**
Adelaide Bank	$4.80 @ 8/8/97	$11.03	10%	5% to 9%	15% to 17%
CBA	$16.45 @ 8/8/97	$38.05	11%	4% to 7%	15% to 17%
Coles Myer	$4.36 @ 10/7/95	$9.36	8%	4% to 8%	12% to 14%
Flight Centre	$1.69 @ 11/1/96	$14.43	27%		
National Bank	$19.56 @ 8/8/97	$31.15	6%	3% to 5%	9% to 11%
Santos	$3.61 @12/10/95	$10.50	11%	4% to 9%	15% to 17%
Suncorp-Met	$6.99 @ 8/8/97	$20.01	14%	5% to 9%	19% to 21%
Woolworths	$2.80 @ 23/7/96	$16.46	22%	6% to 9%	26% to 28%

• Before capital gains tax.

* Based on purchase cost and after 36% or 30% tax paid, depending on which company tax rate applied at the time.

** Averaged over last 9 to 10 years, partially tax paid.

ON THE SUBJECT OF MANAGED FUNDS

If you have been contributing into a managed fund or super-annuation policy that has performed considerably slower than the figures I've shown above, it could be because of hefty – and some-times hidden – management fees involved in having someone else make all of your buy–sell decisions for you. Or it can be due to the structure of the fund itself, which might not be set up in a way that pays its fat returns until the closing years of a fixed agree-ment. Some managed funds are even structured to allow the principle to be devoured for the first few years before they start coughing up with returns that make the deal worthwhile. So always be extremely careful to ensure you understand the risks as well as the structure of any managed funds you may buy into.

Definition Alerts!

Direct investment in shares = Using a stockbroker to buy and sell whichever shares you choose.

Indirect investment in shares = Using managed funds to make smaller, regular contributions. These have much higher management costs which affect your returns.

ON THE SUBJECT OF RISK

It's interesting to note that Telstra and AMP shares are both widely regarded as reasonably priced 'blue-chip' shares and were marketed heavily to mum-and-dad investors at their relevant times of listing. And while many investors made profits from selling these shares later, many other small investors expe-rienced losses. Yet neither company would have been purchased from a prospectus by anyone using the 10-step method in *Your Money: Starting Out and Starting Over* – the method that is also summarised in Chapter 13 of this book – because these two companies both failed to make the 'lower-risk' shortlisting process due to a combination of their projected returns, initial cost, forecasted earnings per share and/or existing debt ratios.

At the other end of the scale, ION – another 'blue-chip' company that did make the shortlisting process at one stage in 2004 using the 10-step method in *Your Money* – went into receivership soon afterwards in the 2004/05 financial year amid widespread accusations that the management board had misinformed the stock exchange as well as its bankers and shareholders about the state of the company and massive blowouts of expansion costs.

So while hyper-conservative selection techniques and the act of spreading your investment coins across a range of investment opportunities can help to keep most of your money safe most of the time, it can't protect each specific investment from focused economic downturns, short-term market fluctuations, misrepresentation or mismanagement by company directors.

> **Rule 12 of the 50 Fun Rules for Success:
> Never stick all your financial eggs in the
> one basket.**

What does this mean for money-tree style of investments that start small and don't deal with enough cash to spread investments over more than one or two types of savings account (until it reaches about $1000 to $2000 and buying shares become an option)? It means patience and planning – patience because the time will come when you *do* have sufficient cash to split investments into wider risk/return alternatives. And planning because you need to know what your options are *before* you consult a professional advisor to ensure that you don't get herded like a lemming toward the latest blue-chip or cash-management fad.

ON THE SUBJECT OF HIGH, LOW AND MEDIUM RETURNS

Every small investor has been sickened from time to time over the last five years by the ads on TV which advertise investment and term deposit returns as being 'generous' if they make it over 3%. What does that make a poor return, for goodness sake? So, aside from needing to look more widely for better opportunities (avoiding the high-risk end of the market, of course), we also need to step back and take a broader look at returns over a longer period as follows:

1. The examples for share investment (page 24) give an indication of how well the best blue chip shares have performed over the last 10 years, as well as how a portfolio of choice blue- and green-chips has almost doubled those returns in the same period, simply by buying and selling a few times to take advantage of cyclical highs and lows.

2. Now compare this to the information made available by ASIC on their website where it's illustrated that Australian shares have grown by an average of 12% to 13% per year over the 50-year period from 1950 to 2000 (assuming no sales occurred to maximise the benefits of peaks and troughs and also assuming that all proceeds were reinvested).

Note: ASIC recommends that any investment offer of 15% or more per year requires a detailed explanation and a second opinion. ASIC also makes clear that the average return from Australian or international shares, property, bonds or cash has never beaten 20% per year in any period during the past 20 years – even during periods of an exciting investing climate. However, this is an average figure across many companies including many companies that were high-risk or did not perform as well as they could have. It is not to be confused with the highly reputable 27% individual success of Flight Centre shares illustrated on page 24 or the 8% to 40% returns mentioned earlier, which are based on relatively conservative shares but rely on buying and selling in order to maximise annual or biennial lows and highs.

Even so, it seems logical that investors should not be considered unreasonable for expecting returns between 10% and 13% over a 20- to 50-year investment. (Assuming that future economic conditions hold no horrific surprises.)

HUNTING THE BETTER RATES

Where do you find cyclically reliable, slightly higher-risk but much higher-return investments?

a. Among the low-income, big-name, popular-brand blue-chip shares.

b. Resource stocks that don't necessarily pay regular dividends, e.g. gold producers, oil prospectors and companies involved in research and development.

c. Some short-term managed funds.

d. Term-of-life savings policies (see definition on page 37), being cautious of those that charge fees and penalties for leaving early.

The only drawbacks for using such investment vehicles for stashing small amounts away regularly like this (and for the example below as well) are fees, with management funds charging regular fees monthly, annually or as a percentage of each contribution, while shares attract purchase and sale fees (usually called entrance and exit fees) including stamp duty and stockbroker fees.

Definition Alerts!

Ordinary share = A teeny part of a big company which can be purchased in batches using a stockbroker who buys and sells shares electronically for you on Australian or international stockmarkets.

Blue-chip share = An ordinary share in a company which has a high purchase price compared to its competitors because it's considered by the big investors to be worth more for being well-established, highly successful and reliable. But blue-chip shares often pay their investors a lower per cent return in dividends each year compared to non-blue-chips, and the growth in value of each blue-chip share is usually slower than a company that has steeper fluctuations.

So, in practice, it's usually wiser to save up your $20 in batches of $2000 using traditional methods like high-interest savings accounts or term deposits before shifting the cash into the higher-earning share packages that can be managed by yourself or by your stockbroker/fundmanager for a fee.

Note: A super-condensed summary of what to look for in investments is included in Chapter 13 for your convenience.

INVESTMENT STRATEGY 3: The relatively fast, conservative income plus growth option

Again using the $20 from the first example, let's examine the results of investing in ordinary shares that increase in capital value at the rate of about 12% a year at the same time as paying dividends at least twice a year worth an average of 7% per year (based on the original purchase price per share).

Projected savings assuming an opening balance of $100, regular payments of $20/fortnight, 7% income from dividends/year which is reinvested, plus 12% annual growth in the underlying value:

Years involved	Contri- butions so far $	7% Dividends earned $	12% Capital growth $	Total accum- ulated $
8	4200	1500	3000	8700
10	5300	2400	5000	12,700
16	8400	7200	17,400	33,000
18	9400	9600	24,500	43,500
21	11,000	14,200	39,400	64,600
30	15,700	38,200	140,900	194,800
40	20,900	88,900	443,800	553,600
50	26,100	199,600	1,473,800	1,699,500
60	31,300	428,600	4,798,700	5,258,600

Note: One of the greatest things about investing in companies which pay dividends is that you can choose companies which pay either fully franked dividends (which is a fancy way of saying that the 'interest' which is paid to you has had 30% tax already paid to the Tax Office for you) or partially franked dividends (where a portion of the tax has been paid). Some companies even pay unfranked dividends (no tax paid on your behalf, therefore you have to pay tax on it, making dividend returns effectively the same as if the investment had been made into a term deposit or savings account with a similar interest rate). So it's important to choose your shares for either growth, income or both, based on:

- what you expect the capital growth to be, based on product quality, company goals, management skills, levels of company debt and state of the economy;
- expectations of dividends, based on company goals and track records in paying them so far, even during harsh economic downturns;
- how much tax is paid on the dividends for you by the company;
- whether shareholder discounts for products or services that you regularly use anyway would compensate for any minor deficiencies in any of the above.

Did you know?

Our family currently has three money trees, one that's 12 years old for our first child, one that's nine years old for our second child and one that's about eight years old, which we started for fun when we realised how much faster they were growing than we expected.

We had to put up with low interest from savings accounts for the first few months after planting each money tree, shifting the money into shares each time we had saved enough to purchase a bundle (sometimes with both boys pooling funds to purchase one batch of shares in the same company).

Eight years ago we decided to top up the younger child's account to equal our older son's account so they'd both get an equal inheritance from our estate if anything happened to us. Due to some of our green-chip investments performing much better than expected, our sons now have money trees worth a little over $22,000 each, even though our small regular contributions (and the once-off top up for younger child) cost an average of only $6500 each.

To be honest, I don't know if the money will eventually be used for university education, first cars or deposits on a first home, because I intend to leave many of those decisions up to them and their circumstances at the time. They may even prefer to take over their portfolios to keep as little money-spinners to help raise their own children. But one thing is sure: it's one heck of a nice feeling to know the money is there and still growing without costing us much by comparison.

3

Financial Planning for the Unborn

Prospective parents have a lot of points to consider when planning the births of their children. Four of the most worrying often include:

1. How much is a child likely to affect our lifestyle and finances?
2. How soon will we need a bigger house and/or car?
3. Can we afford to provide well enough for our child as they grow?
4. How can we afford the major upgrades when it's time?

HOW MUCH WILL A CHILD AFFECT LIFESTYLE AND FINANCES?
Radically, but not as much as your first nightmares would have you believe. And, thankfully, not as much as many financial calculators seem to expect either – at least not as far as your capacity to make extra (albeit smaller) repayments on your car and home loans are concerned. Budgets and official borrowing capacity can be different matters and these will both affect the timing of when you can consider upgrading your home or car.

ADVANCE BUDGETING FOR BABIES
An all-state survey conducted in early 2005 reported that the cost of raising a child from birth to uni had broken the $1,000,000 mark (per child in Sydney) for the first time, with other major cities not too far behind. However, these calculations included about $425,000 in lost wages while raising a child, as well as an average of $45 per week for the child's impact on power bills and increased rent or mortgage repay-

ments. This is a complex and emotional matter, and everyone will weigh up the issues differently and decide on what different sacrifices and priorities to make when they start a family. So there's no need to panic. It's not the cost that matters, so much has how well you deal with it on a week-to-week basis. More general costs for raising a child are available at www.youthfacts.com.au.

HOW SOON WILL WE NEED A BIGGER HOUSE AND/OR CAR?

The timing of the purchase for any new vehicle depends on the obvious aspects of how many seats your existing car has and how reliable it is, versus how many children you plan to have, how soon and how much extra room you will need for pets, groceries and your growing children's friends.

New baby capsules (for infants aged from 0 to six months) and fully adjustable recliners (which are like thrones for children up to two years old) range from $200 to $500 new or $50 to $250 second-hand. Renting the base models costs between $50 and $120 per six months (including a refundable deposit) plus the same again for professional fitting to your vehicle. (For details of who is authorised to fit child restraints, contact the Roads and Traffic Authority in your state.) Later, as they grow, booster seats for older youngsters can be fitted to the vehicle using the existing seat belt. They're much cheaper, too, ranging from $50 to $120.

Great care and planning are needed when deciding whether to buy or rent your baby capsule. Many old brands are no longer considered roadworthy so buying them may be a waste of your time and money, and dangerous.

The upgrading of homes, on the other hand, may be less urgent since children can share rooms quite happily – many even prefer it – until their age draws nearer to double figures and issues of privacy and territory begin to stir. However, affordability of an upgrade to your home decreases dramatically as soon as the bulge in the tummy begins to show.

BABIES VERSUS BORROWING CAPACITY

To illustrate why young families often have their best chances at securing their own home if they arrange the purchase of their first property *before* the tummy bulge begins to show, let's take the example of an ordinary budget-wise couple with moderate monthly net incomes of $2000 each and existing debts for car and credit cards totalling about $20,000.

   Without children, it's not too hard for them to secure a loan with a reputable lender for about $255,000 (assuming they have the deposit and pay 8% interest over 30 years). Of course, unless they're upgrading from an existing property, then finding a larger home for that size of loan may still be fairly tricky. Look what happens to this couple's chances for a loan as soon as children are introduced into the banks' version of the financial equation:

Double income: $2000 each per month (after tax) with $20,000 in existing debts:

Number of dependants	Loan possible with a reputable lender	Minimum repayments per month
0	$255,000	$1870
1	$215,000	$1578
2	$180,000	$1321
3	$145,000	$1064
4	$110,000	$807
5	$75,000	$550
6	$35,000	$257
7	Doh! Bank manager sends apologies and recommends a nice camping ground	

Each child reduces this couple's borrowing capacity by $35,000 to $40,000! Now consider the same couple, if they take a little more time planning their family in order to pay off most of their debts first.

Double income: $2000 each per month (after tax) with no existing debts:

Number of dependants	Loan possible with a reputable lender	Minimum repayments per month
0	$325,000	$2385
1	$290,000	$2128
2	$250,000	$1834
3	$215,000	$1578
4	$180,000	$1320
5	$145,000	$1064
6	$110,000	$807
7	$70,000	$514

Can you see how each child still reduces the couple's borrowing capacity by $40,000 but the absence of $20,000 in other debts increases their borrowing capacity in each case by an average of $70,000? Pretty amazing, hey?

So aside from the fact that budget-wise couples will notice they can usually afford more than what the banks say they can afford in minimum repayments, these examples scream a warning more than ever about the importance of paying off your cars and credit cards *before* attempting to add children into your own budget predictions.

The underlying suggestion in such loan calculations (which, by the way, don't usually permit us to count any income from family payments, child-support payments or lump-sum maternity allowances from Centrelink for having a baby), is that even a breastfed youngster costs between $250 and $300 per month out of our normal pay packets to raise and care for. And that's *on top* of the expenses covered by those other payments! When the true monthly cost for young children – especially for children under five years of age – can often be considerably less without needing to scrimp too much on quality of lifestyle.

However, you'll hear economists from time to time discussing how the loss of income and upgrades to home and cars should be 'charged' to the expense of bearing and raising our children. This works well enough on the macro-planning level for governments, but doesn't help much for a family budget. It's also considerably unfair on the youngster, especially for a family budget where the bottom-dollar has to be balanced against less tangible aspects of the equation, like the emotional pleasure of raising our little munchkins.

Also remember the capital growth on a larger home over the first 16 years of your child's life is likely to 'repay' your pocket for the initial expense of upgrading – many times over! (Unless you over-commit or fail to make small, regular extra repayments over the term of the loan.)

If you operate a business from a home office in the larger home, while parking your larger semi-business car in the larger semi-business garage, it will increase your deductible business expenses making the upgrade(s) even more affordable.

TOP TIPS FOR BABY BUDGETING BEFORE PREGNANCY

Planning budgets to cope with the prospect of babies can stretch as far back as the engagement and decisions of how much to spend on the wedding. Ideally, a couple should not be getting into debt at all in order to celebrate their new path in life together – especially if they plan to go forth and multiply within five years of hitching their wallets together.

Think about it. It's not financially logical to leap backwards into a pit before attempting to climb a mountain. Yet very often couples feel so overwhelmed by the debt of their first mortgage and car purchases that a few extra thousand for the wedding seems inconsequential. But it's important to find a healthy balance between debt and desirable purchases, because every extra $10 paid off your debts during those early stages can save up to $96 over the full term of the loan.

Put another way, every $1000 paid off your major loans before children arrive will save up to $10,000 in interest payments by the time your children are ready to move out. Extrapolate that a little further and you can see how an extra three grand paid off your mortgage before the birth of your first child can mean the difference in being able to afford university fees for them or providing a gift of their first car – or not.

Note: Some readers will argue that the amount of bank interest you can save will be higher if you can pay lump sums off your debts as soon as the money is available. And of course this is true. But in reality, it's more common and much easier to achieve smaller repayments more often.

AGE: MINUS TWO YEARS TO CONCEPTION
The following list provides specific tips and handy hints to help with some of the most under-appreciated budget aspects relating specifically to youngsters prior to birth.

Private health insurance: Check out the cost of top-level health insurance and try to join while you're still in the planning stages for your baby. You can always drop down to cheaper insurance after the baby's born AND you're sure that both you and your baby are 100% healthy. But you can't usually receive ANY benefits from health insurance (either during pregnancy, birth or post-natal) if you join *after* you beome pregnant. *Handy hint:* No gap medical service providers are a welcome relief to struggling families, since they don't charge more for their services than the amount you'd get back from insurance. But you have to make sure they're no-gap providers *before* you make your appointment with them.

Note: Since 1 January 1999, the government has paid a 30% rebate to Australians who pay premiums to an appropriate health fund, but in real terms to family budgets, health insurance is more expensive than ever, even after the rebate has been applied.

Life insurance: Keep your eyes open for term-of-life insurance policies that allow you to re-draw premiums as no-interest loans with no or low penalties for your final agreed payout. These 'life insurance policies with lump sum payouts if you (or your children) don't die by a certain age' were in the process of being phased out over a decade ago. To some extent they've been replaced by certain managed funds and term investments which are advertised as being highly suitable for saving for your child's education at university (or their first car). But the investment industry's version of a fixed-term financial product is more likely to penalise a parent if they need to redraw their premiums during times of financial difficulty (or if their child dies before the date of maturation). The insurance industry's version of the product was vastly superior and whispers suggest the 'old' term-of-life policies may soon be repackaged and re-introduced as a 'new product'. Just beware of the ravenous fees that may be involved!

> **Warning:** Don't be a milking cow for the investment or insurance industries. Always beware of policies which charge fees that devour your promised returns.

Okay, now you're going to think I'm a little zealous with the next two suggestions, but I've done them both myself, and trust me – the cash and intangible benefits work superbly – even if your friends and relatives do laugh themselves silly when you tell them!

Financial year implications: Consider planning the conception and subsequent birth date of your baby with the goal of ensuring the new mum (or stay-at-home dad) has the no-pay portion of their maternity leave (or paternity leave) spread across from one financial year into the next. Why? Because it will usually result in the unpaid parent getting a much bigger tax refund two years in a row (due to the nature of the sliding scale used for tax scales in calculating regular full time salaries). If both parents take extended leave without pay from one financial year into the next, then you'll both usually have fatter tax refunds to look forward to.

Birth-date planning: Planning more than one pregnancy by the method above means you can also save money, stress and hassle with birthday parties later on when your children agree to share one big party, instead of having one each at different times of the year. Less wear 'n' tear on your house as well as your sanity!

AGE: CONCEPTION TO BIRTH
The following tips provide more food for thought for advance planning.

1. Dig out your most treasured money box from your own childhood and set it in pride of place in your baby's nursery. Then for each week of your pregnancy, deposit all the smallest coins from your purse into the money box to save for your child's first bank account.

2. Keep your eyes open for bargain second-hand furniture that's solid and restorable for a low cost and a little elbow grease (e.g. steel prams or timber cabinets, cots etc). Restoring them to sell for a profit – and doing it a few more times to help raise extra cash – can give your budget a welcome boost as well as helping familiarise you with different features involved with many of the different brands, so that by the time your own little tike is born, you can make sure they have the safest and best of each piece you've restored.

3. Try keeping a mental note of the approximate value of all baby gifts given to you by your friends and family. Then try to match dollar for dollar into a savings account to help cover the ever-increasing gaps between Medicare and the cost of regular visits to your GP and specialists (before birth as well as the first two years ex-tummy, which are usually the most hectic). Without your friends and family, you would have spent the money anyway, so doing this – or at least as much as you can afford – is one way of making sure that you don't let the cash slip through your fingers.

4. Don't waste money buying books or videos about parenting too early in your pregnancy when you can borrow them for free from your local library, kindergarten or pre-school (and then use your knowledge to buy only ones that you'll use regularly). You may not have realised it yet, but as soon as your friends and family find out that you're having a baby, you're going to be bombarded with hints, tips and parental advice. Oh, boy, are you ever!

ON THE SUBJECT OF STOCKPILING

Financially speaking, the sooner you begin bargain-hunting and stockpiling all the baby consumables you'll need, the easier it will be on your pocket, especially during any length of time that you'll be away from work without pay. But most new mums-to-be prefer to begin stockpiling consumables as soon as they've waved to the little three- or four-month-old fuzzy foetus through the miracle of ultrasound. By that time, you've usually come to terms with the concept of a new life form taking over your body, or your partner's body, if you happen to be the expectant dad.

> *Special note for dads-to-be:* My husband used to complain that there were never any baby books that made dads feel welcome to read them. So if you're a dad reading this book, you should know that I mean you, too, every time I mention being pregnant, having babies or changing nappies!

Stockpiling too early increases the risk of financial depression associated with haywire hormones and the physical act of placing each baby-related item into your shopping trolley: each pack of nappies can seem like the next brick in building your own padded jail. But honestly, it doesn't matter how prepared you are financially, if hormones run rampant, the simple process of putting a baby's bib into your trolley can reduce the most confident mum to a sobbing wreck in seconds. That's hormones for you. So if it affects you, don't sweat. Just try:

- doing it later, when you're feeling better;
- taking friends to help keep you cheery;
- sending your partner shopping;
- stockpiling cash into a savings account instead.

In any case, when you're ready, you'll need at least five bibs, three pairs of baby socks, three neutral-coloured babysuits (size 000), two sets of baby sheets and pillow cases for the cot, three singlets and the tallest pile of spurp-rags you can scrape together. (Spurp rags are super-soft tea-towels or face washers to hang over your shoulder, use as pillow protectors, face-wipes and emergency nappy padding.) Other consumables that pack nicely into a wardrobe include super-soft tissues, nappy wipes, nipple pads, baby bottles, drink-cups, laundry detergent, bath bubbles, larger-sized clothes, shoes, hats and throw-rugs.

Warning: Don't overstock on nappies, since you won't know what you'll need until you figure out the sensitivity of your baby's skin, and nappies are way too expensive to make mistakes. You'll need about a dozen cloth nappies to get you started in hospital as well as for the first one to three months after you escape. But even the most nature-conscious mum may want to swap to disposables at some stage, even if it's only for trips away from the house.

PLANNING FOR CHILDCARE AND/OR VIABLE ALTERNATIVES

Attendance at childcare is not compulsory and therefore fees are only necessary or helpful if you:

- need or want to get back to work and don't have a close relative who is keen to babysit every day;
- need a break during the week from a challenging or overly-energetic child;
- can't get a placement for your child in a government preschool or kindy AND you feel your child is ready for and/or needs the social interaction with children their age;
- enjoy the greater flexibility or newer facilities at a childcare centre.

Note: in many areas the trend is reversed, with vacancies for children harder to find in the childcare centres.

COSTS

Childcare fees for babies and children aged one to three are usually dearer than for older children because of the much tighter staff-to-child ratio required. (Babies need the greatest level of supervisory care, and therefore by law a carer is able to look after fewer babies than older children.)

And while childcare centres can usually boast of having the best facilities that money can buy, as well as staff who should be dilligent, loving, trained and professional, they also have their downsides, such as greater contact with colds and flu than young children in home-stay situations with other relatives, nannies and smaller circles of friends in the neighbourhood.

Approved 'neighbourhood' childcare centres are therefore popping up in greater numbers in many areas too, with mothers registering their quality homes for regular audits and performing all the required maintenance and improvements to yards, rooms and stairs in order to make them safety compliant so they can run a modest childcare centre from home, rather than returning to work and having the childcare fees eating into *their* income!

Fees otherwise cost between $35 and $85 per child, per day (not counting the 30% childcare rebate, see page 45), with some of the most heavily booked centres charging even higher fees. Parents of more than one child in daycare often see the benefits of hiring a nanny, or sharing a nanny with their neighbours, workmates or nested families.

4

Government Cash After Birth

This chapter deals with the family benefits available through Centrelink and rebates available through the Australian Tax Office for income and expenses related to children. All rates of payment are correct at the time of publication.

CENTRELINK PAYMENTS FROM BIRTH TO JOB SEARCHING

Centrelink makes a number of payments to help fund families through the financial difficulties of raising children as follows. The info is provided here in approximate order of usage.

Family Tax Benefit (Part A) is an annual tax benefit claimed through the Tax Office to help families with the cost of raising children. Payments are made to the parents, guardians, foster parents or grandparents who are responsible for the day-to-day care of the kiddies and/or grandkiddies. FTB(A) is subject to an income test and a residency test, but not an assets test, which means it doesn't matter how many assets you own, but your residency status and the amount of taxable income you earn each year will affect the amount you're eligible to receive. To be eligible, you must have either a dependent child under 21 or a dependent full-time student aged 21 to 24.

Warning: You can't claim FTB(A) for a dependant who is your partner, or aged 16 or over and earning a taxable income of $10,948 or more, or aged between 5 and 15 years (unless they're in full-time study and have a taxable income of less than $10,948), or receiving any Centrelink payment which helps them to find a job.

The base rates for FTB(A) are $44.10 per fortnight for

under-18-year-olds and $59.36 for 18- to 24-year-olds. The
maximum rates of FTB(A) for each child are:
* 18 to 24 years: $59.36 per fortnight
* 16 to 17 years: $44.10 per fortnight
* 13 to 15 years: $173.74 per fortnight
* under 13 years: $137.06 per fortnight
* 0 to 24 years in an approved care organisation: $44.10 per
  fortnight.

Various supplement payments may also be paid in association
with the FTB(A) by the Tax Office at the end of each financial
year in the form of a tax refund or reduced tax bill. These
include:
* **Large Family Supplement** for the fourth and each subsequent child, payable at the rate of up to $9.24 per child per
  fortnight.
* **Multiple Birth Allowance** as a fortnightly payment of
  $111.86 for triplets or $149.10 for quads (or more).
* **Rent Assistance** between $65 and $130 per fortnight if
  you get more than the base rate of FTB(A), pay rent
  privately and can provide evidence of the rental agreement.
  Payments vary depending on how many dependants you
  have and whether you're single or married.

Family Tax Benefit (Part B) is paid either fortnightly or
through the tax system as a lump sum after submitting your tax
records to the Tax Office at the end of each financial year. Or
you can elect an option that allows your employer to deduct less
tax from your paypacket (or your partner's pay packet).

The FTB(B) is subject to an income test, but not an assets
test. Unlike the FTB(A), the primary earner in a partnered
relationship (or a sole parent) is exempt from the income test.

Maximum payment rates are $114.66 per fortnight if your
youngest child is under five years old, or $79.94 per fortnight
if your youngest is between five and 15 years old (or 18 years
while still a full-time student).

Maternity Payment is paid as a lump sum to families following the adoption, birth or stillbirth of a baby, in recognition of the extra costs associated with medical and home expenses. It is not subject to an income test or an assets test – all families are paid the same. It is, however, subject to an Australian residency test.

To be eligible for the payment, claims usually have to be lodged within 26 weeks from the birth or adoption date, with forms being provided to mothers while in hospital or by social workers at the adoption centre.

The Maternity Payment is $3079 per birth (or per child in the event of a multiple birth), with increases (due to inflation) usually taking place in March and September of each year. However, the May 2004 Federal Budget announced Maternity Payment increases to $4000 from 1 July 2006, and to $5000 from 1 July 2008.

And thankfully, Maternity Payment is not counted towards taxable income, family assistance or social security purposes.

Maternity Immunisation Allowance is not subject to an income or assets test and is a one-off lump sum payment of $216.20, payable if:
• your child is fully immunised between 18 and 24 months;
• your child is on a recognised immunisation catch-up schedule;
• your child has an approved exemption from being immunised; or
• your child is stillborn or dies before 24 months, AND you received Maternity Payment for your child.
If you're not being paid Family Tax Benefit (FTB) at the time that your child turns 18 months, you'll need to fill in a fresh claim form for the MIA. All claim forms have to be lodged through the Family Assistance Office, not through the tax system, as in the case of the FTB.

Childcare Benefit is payable if you pay to use approved or registered childcare for one or more of your dependent children, provided that you satisfy certain Australian residency criteria and your child is immunised or exempt from the immunisation requirements. You, and your partner if you have one, must also be working, studying or training if you wish to claim between 20 and 50 hours per week (with some exceptions). The benefit is paid by providing a discount in your childcare fees.

Approved care is provided by most family daycare, long daycare, before and after school care, vacation care and occasional care services, to name a few. It's subject to an income test, but not an assets test, and the benefit can either be paid directly to the childcare service to reduce the fees charged to you, or it can be paid to the parents/guardians as a lump sum after submitting their tax returns at the end of the financial year.

For example, a non-school-aged child in 50 hours of care per week is entitled to a benefit up to $2.88 per hour (up to $144 per week), while payment rates for school-aged children are 85% of the non-school aged rate under the same circumstances.

Registered care, on the other hand, is a service provided by kindergartens, occasional care centres, nannies, grandparents/relatives/friends and some private pre-schools, provided that they're each registered with the Family Assistance Office. The benefit for this is not subject to either an income test or an assets test, but it's only payable to your bank account after you're able to provide receipts of payment for childcare to the Family Assistance Office.

The parent of a non-school-aged child in 50 hours of work-related care is due a reimbursement of up to $0.483 per hour ($24.15 per week), with rates for school-aged children being 85% of the non-school-aged rate under the same circumstances.

Youth Allowance is subject to an Aussie residency test as well as an income test and an assets test. Assuming your child passes all tests, payments to parents/guardians for young people range from $178.70 per fortnight for a single student aged under 18 who is still living at home and has no children up to $427.80 per fortnight for a single person with children. The allowance is paid as a fortnightly payment into a parent's bank account (with special payments for migrants from a non-English speaking background).

Austudy Payment aims to provide financial assistance if you're aged 25 years or older AND you can meet certain Aussie residency criteria AND you're either studying or undertaking a new apprenticeship full-time AND your course of study or apprenticeship is approved by Centrelink. Maximum payments vary between $326.50 and $427.80 per fortnight depending on whether you're single or partnered and have children or not. The payment is subject to both an income AND an assets test. People who are eligible to receive payment may also be entitled to Advance Payments between $250 and $500, with many provisos for use and repayments, or Fares Allowance – which aims to help tertiary students cope with the costs of travelling while living away home in order to study, usually only paid as a one-way or return ticket per year.

Pharmaceutical Allowance is a non-taxable payment of $5.80 per fortnight for single people and $2.90 a fortnight for each eligible member of a couple ($5.80 combined) provided that recipients meet certain Aussie residency criteria.

Handy hint: Keep records of how much you pay for prescriptions each year, or shop from the same pharmacy all the time to ensure they keep records for you. Then, when you've paid for 52 scripts through the Pharmaceutical Benefits Scheme (PBS) in a calendar year, all PBS medicines are free for the rest of the year.

Remote Area Allowance is not taxable and is not subject to either an income or assets test, but it does reduce the amount of zone rebate you'd be able to claim in your tax return each year. Single people are entitled to an RAA of $18.20 per fortnight, while couples receive $15.60 each plus $7.30 for each dependent child.

Assistance for Isolated Children is payable if your family home is geographically isolated from a suitable government school, or your child has a proven health-related or educational requirement that can't be helped locally AND has to board away from home in a school, hostel or rental property. It is also payable if your family has to maintain a second home so your child can attend their school daily, AND/OR your child studies full-time at an approved distance education institution. There are several allowances for isolated children:

* *Boarding Allowance*, which consists of a non-income-tested basic rate of $6000 per year plus an additional allowance of $1069 per year, subject to the parental income test and actual boarding costs;
* *Second Home Allowance* of $174.79 per fortnight per student, limited to three students per family;
* *Distance Education Allowance* of $3000 per year for primary or secondary students;
* *Assistance for Isolated Children Pensioner Education Supplement* of $62.40 per fortnight, payable only for students under 21 years of age who receive a Disability Support Pension or Parenting Payment (Single) AND who are studying below secondary level.

Jobsearch Allowance – the current official name is Newstart Allowance – helps you survive financially until you find work with a fortnightly payment of $360 to $437, depending on whether you're single, partnered, have children or are aged over 60. It's only available to people who are over 21, unemployed and not involved in any kind of strike or industrial action. Newstart Allowance is subject to income and assets tests, and it may be deferred if you have 'cash liquid assets' over $2500, which includes money in bank accounts and shares, among other easily-cashed-in assets, so always encourage your young adult child to contact Centrelink BEFORE they resign from their current job, or they could be in for a nasty surprise regarding their eligibility for payments. However, if your child happens to be eligible, then other payments sometimes payable in association with Newstart Allowance include:

- A $104 Employment Entry Payment to help with costs of getting a new job;
- A $208 Education Entry Payment to help with training to improve prospects of getting a new job;
- Pharmaceutical Allowance if you get sufficiently sick during periods of unemployment;
- Additional payments if participating in a Work for the Dole program;
- Rent Assistance, Remote Area Allowance and/or Telephone Allowance;
- A Health Care Card to help reduce the cost of regular medical expenses.

TAX REBATES AND OFFSETS

There are a range of reductions to the tax which is taken from your pay packet. They include:

- **Dependent rebates**, depending on whether you're able to claim as a dependent either a spouse, child under 16, spouse and child under 16, student under 25, childminder/housekeeper, parent, spouse's parent or an invalid relative as well as how long any of these were your dependent during the year and their own incomes (also known as their separate net incomes). For example, in the financial year ended June 2004, you would only be eligible for a dependent rebate if the separate net income earned by your dependent was less than $6422.
- **Zone rebates** depending on which remote area zone of Australia you worked in during the financial year, and if you lived/worked in a defined remote area zone for less than 183 days, then it will also depend on your prior year zone and claim details.

5

The Toddling Years – From Birth to Pre-pre-school

This chapter handles two major topics:
1. Expenses relating to children from birth until pre-school.
2. Investments and opportunities made possible by savings in expenses.

I've included an assortment of the weirdest, most fun and profitable short cuts to coping with your own finances, as well as suggestions for paving your child's financial highway to success in ways that you may have grossly underestimated. (Or never imagined!) Children are also beginning to talk (and talk back) by this stage, so now is the perfect opportunity to introduce the basics of money and its uses for good, while warning against its uses for evil.

SURVIVING MATERNITY/PARENTAL LEAVE

Terminology varies between workplaces and industries, with the majority of definitions of maternity leave being leave granted to the mother for the purposes of having a baby, while parental leave is non-gender-biased leave for exactly the same purpose and both can be applied to either the birth or adoption of a child.

If mothers are sick immediately prior to birth or adoption they may also 'charge' a portion of their parental or maternity leave against any sick leave or holidays owing to them.

Both full-time and part-time employees who've had at least 12 months continuous service for an employer are entitled to parental leave, while for casual employees it's regular and systematic engagement of services for at least one year (making them 'long-term casuals') that makes them eligible. (Technically speaking, casual employees who aren't long-term casuals, piece-workers and seasonal staff aren't entitled to parental leave, but since they are casual and can therefore often be replaced temporarily by more casuals, it's a rare situation where an employer would risk losing a good casual worker by not granting them leave.)

Parental leave applies equally to married and unmarried couples and there's no age limit. A pregnant employee is entitled to an unbroken period of up to 52 weeks unpaid maternity leave for the child's birth. But many women take less than this, simply because the financial pressures (and some-times the yearning to have a conversation with someone who doesn't gurgle) drive them back to the workplace within a year.

Some women take about six weeks off either side of the baby's due date — especially where duties and workplace safety concerns make it unsafe for them to remain working. The mini-mum required by law, however, is one week's leave before and after birth.

PAID MATERNITY LEAVE

This is still a dream for women in many industries; however, for those employers who have taken it on board as a tool for helping them retain their long-term, fully-trained staff, it is often offered in a mix of two formats: some of the period able to be taken on full pay and some of it paid at half-rates over double the time. In either case, it's a welcome relief to the family budget and can sometimes even be taken as a lump sum. But beware of earning too much income in one financial year, only to earn much less in the following year: you could end up paying more tax than you need to.

SURVIVING DAY-TO-DAY COSTS

If you have to say goodbye to one parent's full-time income while raising a child, you'll notice the impact on your family budget of the loss or partial loss of money you've grown accustomed to spending. At the same time, additional costs will bombard your pile of bills, such as a need for a bigger house, unit or car. Here are my handy hints for being able to afford raising the little tikes well enough to set financial foundations.

- **Visit your local pharmacy to join their free baby club** and see an early childhood nurse – with the added bonus of receiving free promotional goodie bags and baby photos that aren't usually available at hospital- or local-council-based clinics. Joining as soon as you're pregnant can provide you with additional information sessions.

- **Advertise for the clothes and baby furniture** you need on the free noticeboards at kindergartens and pre-schools, where some mothers are discovering they don't need their baby things anymore. Often you'll find mothers generous enough to throw in a few extras.

- **Breastfeed for as long as possible** to save hundreds of dollars on formula, bottles and sterilising equipment. It's also a major convenience and time-saver for helping to maintain independence (priceless!).

- **Stockpile milk powder whenever it's on special** by marking used-by dates in thick black pen on the lids and ensuring you store powder in a cool, dry cupboard to avoid spoiling – even when the powder is stored in a sealed tin. And be careful in going too far out of your way just to buy it for a few cents cheaper at another store, since the fuel involved may end up costing you more than you'll save.

- **Take care in size and style selection of clothes.** For premmy babies you can buy *gorgeous* comfortable clothes at the flea market, if you don't mind shopping amongst dolls of the 'cabbage patch' size. And they're not only a fraction of the cost, they're also handmade with love.

- **Get involved in a hand-me-down network** of the older-cousin or next-door-neighbour variety. Some clothes wear out so fast, there's no point, but for durable, quality wear (especially for the pre-crawlers), choosing dual-sex colours can mean up to three or four children can get use out of them –

or at least help you sell them faster second-hand for a better resale price if you don't have anyone else to pass them on to.

- **Placing iron-on mending patches** inside the knees of trousers and jeans of crawlers to reinforce the material while the long pants are still brand new will usually lengthen the life of pants up to three times!

- **Mashed leftover vegetables** from adult meals can be frozen in ice-cube trays and microwaved to make instant baby food, preferably unseasoned and unsalted, of course, although I've been guilty of using lightly salted mashed potato and the kids have thrived on it. Two to four cubes are the equivalent of one small tin or bottle of baby food. This can save you up to $3.50 per baby meal.

- **Wash clothes and dishes in their maximum-sized loads** to help save on washing powder, water, power and time. Come on, smack your fingers. You know you can do better with this one! I know you have to wash every day with a young spurpy baby, but you have other things you can slip in as well to maximise your efficiency, don't you?

PRE-POCKET MONEY AND NON-CASH REWARDS

During the toddling and prior-to-school years, a child's under-standing of money and value are beginning to grow even without guidance, simply by watching parents handle cash transactions at shops as well as swap money between wallets, withdraw cash from ATMs and deal out tuckshop orders or pocket money to older brothers and sisters.

On the one hand, you want them to develop into respons-ible, financially literate consumers. But on the other hand, you can maximise their appreciation of non-cash rewards by 'pay-ing them' for personal achievements or helping you around the house with non-monetary pleasures, such as a special visit to Grandma's or a sleep-over night for their friends. Or perhaps even a visit to the park, your nearest McDonald's playgym or town library. Art galleries and museums usually offer free entry with special activity areas for children too.

FIRST CASH CONCEPTS

The first few times you catch your young child watching those magical papers and coins change hands, it's important that you take a moment to explain what money is and where it comes from, tracing back along the line of stewardship from wallet to bank account to employer to bank again, and before that to the Australian Mint in Canberra where they're created – making sure that you use the word stewardship instead of ownership, since money is just a trading token that represents our wealth and is actually owned by the government which issues it.

Other opportunities to discuss the chain of stewardship may arise when:

- you receive cash that includes damaged notes or coins, which gives you the opportunity to discuss the legal responsibility to ensure that money doesn't get damaged while you're looking after it, as well as your obligation to return the cash to your bank at the next opportunity;
- you receive coins from other countries by accident, which also provides the opportunity to discuss value of coins between different countries. For example, a New Zealand $2 looks and feels a lot like an Australian $1, but is usually worth somewhere in between.

PROGRESSING TO POCKET MONEY

Children with older siblings who earn pocket money will desire the 'gold commodity' sooner, some as early as two years old, while firstborns may be difficult to motivate into doing chores for cash rewards until they're older. Just like learning to talk, each child develops differently, and it's quite common for many to prefer non-cash rewards for as long as they see greater value in them. But don't be discouraged if you think your child is not 'getting it' quickly enough – the concept of working for cash rewards, that is. Consider the options: a child who prefers their rewards as time spent at a park, museum or library versus a child who chases the chink of gold coins into their piggy banks (especially if they have no particular goal purchase in mind). I know which *I* prefer, and it's not the coin-crazed child.

It's the concept of working for a reward that's important during these early stages. The introduction of cash into the equation is secondary. And as far as your own child is concerned, you'll know it's time to switch from non-cash to cash rewards when you hold up a coin, ask them to make their bed or tidy their toys and they run to obey.

Did you know?
Goal setting is a crucial skill for the process of working toward a savings target. It's also a skill that's encouraged extensively from many angles throughout the education system from grades K to 12, including targets for home-work, maths, reading, sport and special projects.

BANK ACCOUNT VS. PIGGY BANK/COIN SOCK
For toddlers and pre-preschoolers, there's a great deal more satisfaction to be had (and relived daily) from keeping pocket money at home in piggy banks, secret safes or money socks or gloves, than from depositing it into bank accounts where they may feel as if they'll never see it again.

Receiving a novelty piggy bank, or making one of your own out of self-hardening clay, plaster of Paris moulded over balloons or funny faces stitched onto socks or gloves, also adds to the fun, pride and sense of achievement. Keeping small amounts of cash at home (up to $10 per pre-schooler, $50 for primary schoolers and $100 for high-schoolers) also:

- allows opportunities for children to make emergency cash loans to parents for unexpected expenses when there are no ATMs around, with interest payable to the kids;
- provides greater opportunities for kids to practice their cash-counting skills. For example, once they've earned an assortment of coins and notes, most kids like to count them regularly to make sure they don't go missing by accident.

BANK ACCOUNTS

Some banks allow children to open their own accounts as soon as they're able to draw a mark that resembles a signature, while others require a parent to open the account in trust for the child until they're old enough to operate the account for themselves.

The top age limit for a child also varies from bank to bank, with some allowing children to progress to card-holding accounts after their 16th birthdays, while others may permit a child as young as 11 or 12 to have sole access to their account, provided a parent signs an initial authority form giving their permission and consenting to remain responsible for any debts or legal damages incurred.

Warning: Although bank accounts for children usually have no or low fees (compared with similar banking products for adults), they also pay notoriously abysmal interest rates, ranging from 0.01% up to around 6%. I'll never forget the look on my son's face when he saw that his friend's bank account of $1000 had earned a total of $8 for the year, while his own investment portfolio which was worth $100 less (by way of stockmarket shares joint-owned with his brother but held in trust by the lowest-income-earning parent at the time) had increased in value by over $400, not counting the $90 he'd earned in tax-paid dividends.

Handy hint: Even if you don't invest in shares, you can still help your child achieve higher returns than most children's savings accounts by using a suitable adult bank account (with high interest and no fees for low usage) or an online savings account (with even higher interest because it can only be accessed electronically). It doesn't really matter if the child doesn't officially have their name on the passbook or statement. For the extra income they'll earn, it can be worth it to write their name on the passbook manually, even when the income is taxed as if it belonged to the adult. (See also page 58.)

One of the first decisions you'll have to make is which type of savings account your child will benefit from the most during the earliest stages of cash saving. Part of that decision will involve a choice between:

- allowing the child to keep the account in their own name;
- holding a trust account for the child(ren) in your name (or the names of both parents);
- holding savings accounts, term deposits or other investments in your own name (or names of both parents) and keeping in mind which child the account(s) are intended for, with instructions for correct distribution described in your will to ensure each account goes to the appropriate child in the event of your death.

Did you know?

Set-up costs for other types of investments like shares and managed funds mean that you usually need to save at least $1000 before investing in managed funds or $2000 if investing directly into stockmarket shares. (See also page 58 for exceptions.) But in either of these advanced methods of 'growing' your child's savings, the child will have to be over 16 years of age if they wish to own the investments in their own names. Otherwise the investment-style savings will usually need to be set up 'in trust' for the child, which means the accounts will be held predominantly in the name(s) of one or both parents with earnings added to the taxable income for those parents each year.

Accounts, opportunities and rules about ages vary greatly from bank to bank so it pays to shop around when you're ready to choose.

Warning: Once a child has authority to use an account (or keycard on their account) in their own name, parents will not usually be able to make phone inquiries into those accounts any more, even if the account had originally been opened as a trust account.

TAX IMPLICATIONS FOR CHILDREN'S BANK INTEREST

It's a terrible situation. On the one hand, national initiatives are admirably encouraging children and young adults to increase their financial literacy skills as rapidly as possible, while on the other hand, the tax thresholds for income earned from investments by minors is akin to hitting them with a big fat stick if they try to put their knowledge to use before getting a job (or cutting the cake on their 18th birthday).

For example, under present tax thresholds, Australians under 18 (the legal definition of a minor) are only allowed to earn $417 tax free before they start losing two thirds of their earnings in tax. Yes – TWO THIRDS! If your child earns more than $417 during a financial year without physically working for it (for example, from bank interest, dividends from shares or distributions from family trusts), then they will have to pay a shocking 66% tax on the amount they earn between $417 and $1445, plus 47% tax on any amount earned over $1445!

These horribly discouraging tax rates were supposed to be intended to stop parents from splitting their income and diverting it to their children to take advantage of lower tax rates. But with each new Federal Budget and increasing goals from both parties aiming to encourage Australians to improve financial literacy for their children (including the buying and selling of shares), as well as encouraging us to save for our future health, education and superannuation needs, we can hope that someone 'up top' will soon see how ridiculous these low limits are and propose changes to the youth tax rates and thresholds to bring sanity back to the taxes on long-term savings for – and with – our children.

Exceptions: Children's income is exempted from the 66% tax rules – and taxed at the same rate as an adult – if the income is:

• earned by physically working for it as an employee, active partner in a partnership or through their own business;
• earned through a disability support pension, orphan pension or rehabilitation allowance;

- related to a child who is disabled (physically or mentally and either permanently or for long periods);
- for a child who is in the care of someone who receives a carer allowance;
- money or property received as an inheritance;
- rental income from property transferred to the minor as a result of an inheritance or family break-up;
- compensation for injuries or money from superannuation or pension fund benefits;
- net capital gains from disposal of any property or investments mentioned above.

Other provisos and provisions do apply, so if your child is likely to earn more than $417 in the coming financial year, contact your accountant or the Tax Office as soon as possible, so you can ensure the accounts and income are set up to keep the Tax Office happy at the same time as lawfully minimising the tax impact on the interest earned by saving for your children and their futures.

6

Planning Education Costs and Savings from Kindy to Uni

ON THE SUBJECT OF PLANNING AHEAD FOR EDUCATION COSTS

Wow! What a mammoth topic when you're trying to plan ahead from kindy to uni, but thankfully it's much less complicated when you have a broad cross-section of the main opportunities and options laid out at your fingertips. Here are some of my favourites, with approximate costs provided just for rough indicative purposes. As an even rougher rule of thumb, you can expect these costs to double every seven to 10 years due to inflation (remembering that your savings goes up too if you invest wisely along the way in shares or property).

KINDERGARTEN/PRE-SCHOOL (AGES THREE TO FIVE YEARS)

Enrolment is not compulsory, but due to popularity, enrolments are usually taken two to four years prior to the starting date, or from birth in very busy areas. A kindergarten or pre-school (different states call them different things) differs from a childcare centre in that it has a fully structured learning curriculum – even finger-painting and 'free-range' independent exploration sessions. Childcare is more like a professional playground with structured learning introduced into the program to help assist children into the pre-school-style environment.

Fees range enormously from kindy to kindy and state to state depending on the number of children attending (which affects how much funding the kindy gets from the state government), as well as the number of grants they receive per year, the success rate of their management committee from year to year, whether it's a government, private or community kindergarten, and whether or not parents vote to pay fees (or a flat contribution levy subsidised by fundraising). Other factors include how many days per week your child attends and how many hours per day. Prices may range from $15 per part-day to $85 per full-day, with the underlying value of prices (not counting discounts for achieving fundraising targets) remaining roughly comparable to the nearest childcare centre, since they officially compete.

Kindergartens are often managed by committees of parents – which usually means flexibility in the program – so if you need more or fewer days for your child, depending on what you can afford, then don't be afraid to ask for changes to suit your situation. If they have a waiting list, it can help them get more children into programs at the same time as catering to those many three- or four-year-olds who aren't ready for full-time kindy, five days a week.

PRIMARY SCHOOL (AGES FIVE TO 11)

Compulsory schooling begins! For government schools the costs can be almost negligible to parents – certainly when compared with the costs of community or private kindergartens and childcare! Some government school fees (not counting books or uniforms) come in at less than $20 per child – and even that's optional!

Private primary school is quite another matter, however, with costs varying between $1100 and $7500 per year! (Not counting any uniforms, books or other resource materials which may be needed.) Costs also increase in accordance with the student's age, with some schools from both government and private sectors also charging a flat textbook levy to students to 'hire' textbooks instead of having to buy them each year.

SECONDARY SCHOOL (EX-PRIMARY SCHOOL TO AGE 18)

Public secondary schools typically range from a flat fee of between $110 and $330 per year, with some of the cheapest

---

Did you know?

Wherever fees are charged for private education centres, it's nearly always possible to apply for a reserved scholarship placement with whole – or partial – fees subsidised after gaining approval of the board of directors (usually based on a combination of academic merit, good behaviour and financial need). So if you suspect your child may qualify, always ask about two years in advance about the application process and/or test required.

---

rates available in Queensland due to the reduction of fees by the state-operated 'textbook and resource allowance' worth $85 to students in grades 8 to 10 and $190 for senior students (increased annually and paid directly to the schools to help minimise paperwork, hassle and administrative costs).

Tuition fees for private secondary schools are usually at least 10% higher each year than for primary school, and are often $4000 to $11,000 per year with some schools charging even more!

For both public and private secondary schools, uniforms, books and other resources can cost families between $500 and $3000 extra per year – although that may include a laptop computer with software, net connection and tech support!

TAFE COLLEGES (AGES 15 TO ADULT)

TAFE colleges can cater for students from 15 years, overlapping with the last three years of secondary school to help accommodate students who can't finish full-time study at high school and wish to complete an adjusted certificate course which better suits their individual needs, including senior certificates for semi-intellectually handicapped persons, apprenticeship training, traineeship courses, workplace training, certificate courses or a TAFE Diploma. Fees range from $110 to $1500 per year, not always counting the course materials, student union fees and other incidentals.

APPRENTICESHIPS AND TRAINEESHIPS (AGES 15 TO ADULT)
These may suit students with a talent for hands-on manual-style trades, making anything from cakes to bricks, and cars to bridges. Employers are offered government subsidies to take on new apprentices, but some trades have preferences for students who've completed their senior certificates – as is the case with electrical trades.

Most apprenticeships last four years with training provided by the employer, while traineeships for other vocations can take much less time – and both courses of study may often be conducted wholly in the workplace with tutors touring to visit their students.

Each state has an education department that can provide you with details of courses available specifically in your area. However, training is also co-ordinated on a national basis, so help is also at hand by contacting Group Training Australia on 1800 819 747 or www.newapprentice ships.gov.au.

Training costs are usually paid by the employer, including time off work to attend lessons, tuition fees, textbooks, tools, safety gear and/or union fees.

UNIVERSITY (AGES 17 TO ADULT)
At current rates of HECS fees (discussed in more detail on page 66), typical costs for a course of study at a university for a year (not counting course materials and union fees) can range between $4000 and $6000 for an undergraduate degree or even higher for a Masters or PhD. But fees vary from uni to uni, as well as from state to state and subject to subject. So see page 68 for a snapshot of costs before contacting the university that interests you the most, and use the following guide to potential scholarships, bursaries and fellowships to help widen your opportunities.

SCHOLARSHIPS, BURSARIES AND FELLOWSHIPS
A wide range of scholarships and bursaries are available to students in all states, administered by each education department.

Did you know?
One of the most helpful and comprehensive search engines for uni scholarships is at www.myfuture.edu.au.

Some are based on merit demonstrated in existing subjects, while others may be granted on grounds of financial hardship. The following list of opportunities in each state is by no means exhaustive, since a wide range of specialist and private colleges also offer their own scholarships.

PRIMARY AND SECONDARY SCHOOL SCHOLARSHIPS
- In Victoria, grants are available for grades 4 through to uni through the Coordinator of Student Scholarships. Contact: (03) 9637 3137 or www.eduweb.vic.gov.au/scholarships/
- A range of music scholarships for NSW students are available. Contact: (02) 9744 9233 or www.musicteachers.com.au
- For Northern Territory opportunities contact: (08) 8901 4909 or www.deet.nt.gov.au/training/events/scholarships_bursaries.shtml
- The Australian Council for Educational Research (ACER) provides a range of annual scholarship tests for some primary schools and/or first year entry into various secondary schools around the country. Registration forms are often available in the second last year before starting at the new school, with tests usually held toward the beginning of the year before they start at their next school. Contact: (03) 9277 5555 or www.acer.edu.au.

TERTIARY COMMONWEALTH SCHOLARSHIPS
Each year the Commonwealth Government sponsors over 10,000 students to help meet the costs of their tertiary education. This assistance takes the form of Commonwealth Education Costs Scholarships (CECSs) and Commonwealth Accommodation Scholarships (CASs), as well as multiple

exemptions from student fees/contributions, international scholarships and scholarships for postgraduate or undergraduate research, outlined as follows:

- **Commonwealth Education Costs Scholarships (CECSs)** aim at helping a handful of the estimated 26,000 full-time students from low socio-economic backgrounds, plus approximately 2500 full-time Indigenous students, who commence university studies each year with a scholarship of $2000 per student per year for up to four years to assist with education costs. In 2004, over 2500 new CECSs were provided with a target to double this by 2008 at a total cost of $128 million over five years.

- **Commonwealth Accommodation Scholarships (CASs)** are to help as many as possible of the 10,000 students from rural and isolated areas, many of whom are from low socio-economic and/or Indigenous backgrounds and have to move away from home for their tertiary education. Grants per student are $4,000 per year for up to four years, with 3000 CASs paid in 2004, rising steadily to a target of over 3500 new scholarships per year by 2008.

EXEMPTIONS FROM STUDENT FEES OR CONTRIBUTIONS

From 2005, the compulsory fees made standard by the Higher Education Support Act (2003) may be exempted by education providers, however funding for this is at the expense of each relevant education provider. New changes from 2005 also mean that exemption scholarships will no longer be treated as income for the purposes of ABSTUDY or pensions/allowances from Centrelink or Veterans Affairs.

INTERNATIONAL SCHOLARSHIPS

There's an increasing range of scholarships available for Australian students to study overseas, from Turkey to Switzerland, Malaysia to the UK. Contact individual universities or IDP Education Australia for more details: www.idp.com/students/scholarships.

Did you know?

Each university offers their own range of scholarships, bursaries and/or fellowships and so do many major industries. For instance, the computer industry offers a range of scholarships via various universities in every state (through the Australian Computer Society Foundation Trust Fund). Contact: (02) 9299 3666 or www.acsfoundation. com.au/ scholarships_current.cfm.

The federal government also offers scholarships specific to various trades, for example the rural health division has scholarships available to trainee nurses, pharmacists and other medical staff as encouragement to get better services into the outback. Contact Rural Health via the Central Office: 1800 020 103 or www.health.gov.au.

Handy hint: When hunting for scholarships in a foreign country, always contact their embassy nearest to you in Australia for details, especially if you don't have Internet access. At least the phone calls are cheaper!

WHAT ARE HECS, SLE, PELS AND HELP?

HECS – Higher Education Contribution Scheme – is the payment for subjects made by students to universities in association with each Student's Learning Entitlement (SLE), which is an entitlement for all Aussie citizens, New Zealanders and holders of a permanent residency visa to have access to a Commonwealth supported placement for up to seven years of full-time study (or the part-time equivalent). Changes following a review in 2002, phased in between 2005 to 2008, make things a little more complicated. For example:

• From 1 January 2005, PELS grants (loans made to students under the Postgraduate Education Loan Scheme to help pay for course costs) are called FEE-HELP and will be made available to undergraduate students as well as postgraduates, with changes to obligations for repayment to go along with the raising of the maximum loans now available up to $50,000 – not sure if that's good news or bad. More like a double-edged sword, since getting deeply into debt before you start your adult life makes it an awful lot tougher to get ahead financially as a new professional, rather than 'doing-it-tough' to cope as well as you can as a uni student. ***Warning:*** You don't have to borrow the whole $50,000 if you don't need it.

- From 1 June 2006, any HECS debt you've accumulated will be re-named a HELP debt. This debt will be added to any FEE-HELP debt and from then on will be known under the one banner as a HELP debt. The payment and repayment options (of being able either to pay fees upfront to get a discount or defer payments until after you're earning sufficient income to be able to pay them off) still exist, but these are now called HECS-HELP. The discount available for upfront payment of fees will drop from 25% to 20%, although the minimum required upfront payment in order to get the discount will remain at $500.

- Students who commenced their continuous studies under HECS arrangements prior to 1 January 2005 will be subject to special conditions for all payments until completion of their course (or the end of 2008, whichever comes the soonest), provided that they contact their education provider and notify them accordingly by filling out the appropriate HECS-HELP forms. Details of special arrangements, which are a mix of the old and new schemes, are available from each relevant education provider.

- In deciding how much income a student can earn before repayment of HECS (or a portion of HECS) becomes compulsory, the threshholds have also been raised from $35,000 in the financial year 2004/05 to $36,184 in 2005/06.

- A little bad news: from 1 January 2005, the bonus for making 'voluntary' extra repayments on your debts (electing to make repayments before increased income or other circumstances makes it compulsory) has dropped from 15% to 10%.

ANNUAL TERTIARY EDUCATION COSTS

The following table illustrates annual course costs per year without discounts or bonuses as described above.

For more information about HECS, SLE, PELS or HELP:

- call the personal tax infoline on 13 28 61;
- call the HECS accounting unit on 1300 650 225;
- check out the new website at www.goingtouni.gov.au.

THE GRAND TOTAL

Are you sitting down? If you're planning on private education for your children all the way from childcare through to a seven year course at uni, then you'd better be sitting down, especially if you don't take advantage of any discounts, scholarships,

Course	Student fees	Government contribution
National priorities courses (e.g. nursing, education)	$0 – $3847	Nursing: $7116 Education: $9511
Band 1 (foreign languages, humanities, behavioural science, social studies, visual & performing arts)	$0 – $4808	Humanities: $4078 Behavioural science, social studies: $6475 Languages, visual & performing arts: $8869
Band 2 (e.g. built environment, accounting, computing, mathematics, economics, administration,	$0 – $6849	Accounting, admin, econs & commerce: $2420 Maths & stats: $4817 Computing, built environment, health: $7212

Course	Student fees	Government contribution
commerce, statistics, health, science, engineering, surveying, agriculture)		Engineering, science, surveying: $12,003 Agriculture: $15,996
Band 3 (e.g. law, dentistry, medicine, veterinary science)	$0 – $8018	$1472 for law courses and $15047 for the others

bursaries or careful money management of fees along the way. You're staring down the barrel of a cost per child of up to $250,000!

At the other end of the scale (choosing public education and entering the workforce after school) it can be much closer to $10,000 inclusive of books and uniforms, or even less for students who earn bursaries or discounts. Obviously, you can't plan the winning of scholarships, but what you can do is plan towards a happy medium of combining government and private education that provides the most affordable and opportunity-providing options to suit your own family and the needs and personal goals of your child.

HOW WILL I AFFORD IT?
In a national Newspoll survey in May 2001, a mix of 1,200 parents and grandparents revealed a worrying trend that although 85% held high hopes that their children or grandchildren would undertake post-secondary education, more than 66% had no idea how they were going to pay for it.

It's fundamental, gang. You know this by now, and if you don't then go back to Chapters 1 to 3. You put savings away, or you make savings from somewhere else in order to put it away – it's the discipline that's the problem! *Oh boy*, isn't it?

FINDING SAVINGS IN A STRANGLED BUDGET

Of course I know how hard it can be to live from pay to pay. It's downright demoralising at times, but the good news is that help is at hand! It's quite obvious that if you're going to save and invest money for – and with – your children, then you have to be able to put your hands on some spare money first. So what strategies can you use on an already tight budget?

1. Give yourself a coffee-break budget makeover by using the simple-as-it-gets budget on page 116, or use the advance budget makeover from *Your Success in Five Years or Less* and by the time you've finished your coffee and two chockie biscuits, you should have found between $50 and $250 that's been secretly slipping through your fingers each fortnight as part of inefficient use of your lunch-money, over-indulgences in lotto or magazines as well as inappropriate or lazy use of the best features in your mortgages, overdrafts, EFTPOS, bill savings account and credit cards.

2. Now you can look wider to help minimise interest on your minor debts. Consolidating them into a cheaper credit card with an interest-free period can typically save you $80 to $150 in the first two months depending on how much you owe on an average day. For example, if you owe $5000 in debts that are costing you 19% interest, that's:

   > $5000 × 0.19 ÷ 365 days in a year × 55 days in a nice long interest free period on a new credit card = $143.15 SAVINGS in the first 55 days using the new card.

   > . . . And if the new card has a lower interest rate than your old card too – let's say 6% for the sake of an example – then for every $1000 you still owe while paying off the rest, you save:

   > $1000 × (0.19 − 0.06) ÷ 365 × 7 = 36 cents per day (or $10.70 in savings per month for every $1000)

So the first 55 days you'll save $143.15

Plus the next month you'll save $53.50 (for 5 lots of $1000 approximately)

= nearly $200 kick-start to your savings in the first quarter.

Or you could try cutting back on chocolate biscuits or other unnecessary snack treats to save $3 to $6 per week for an extra $72 in the same period.

3. Using a similar principal as step 2 above, you could 'park' all of your bill-savings money and cash for groceries into your credit card to reduce the amount of interest you're accruing. These savings could be shared fifty-fifty between your children's financial futures and your credit repayments.

4. If you indulge in too much beer, scotch or cigarettes, then you need to see page 172 for an example of how quitting your pack-a-day habit (or the equivalent value in other naughty habits or non-necessities) can save up to $150,000 off your mortgage interest over the next 30 years – and most of that occurring during the next 18 years (between now and when your hypothetical new baby graduates from high school). This means there's a high chance of you solving most of your savings and investment dilemmas right there.

Setting up automatic deductions – either from your bank account or debited directly from your paypacket is another major way to make saving easier. You rarely miss money that you don't see, so it helps to avoid the regular procrastination over which bill deserves the spare coins more from the leftovers of your regular paypacket. But where do you put those small regular savings? Well, you have two options:

1. The cash money-tree system described in Chapter 2, saving small amounts until they accrue to be big enough for investments in term deposits and/or shares. In this case you'd pay tax on a year-by-year basis on your annual income from the portfolio;

2. Investing in a managed fund. Specifically, one that's designed for education savings, set up to take advantage of tax benefits and government incentives and not taxed until the money is withdrawn.

EDUCATION SAVINGS PLANS (ESPS)

Quite an appropriate acronym for a long-term savings account actually, since it would take the talent of 'ESP' – Extra Sensory Perception – to know with any close degree of accuracy how much is going to be in a long-term investment by the time you reach the end of it.

But we won't hold that against managed funds, nor this particular variety of managed fund either, since that's the dilemma confronting any kind of non-guaranteed long-term investments. It simply isn't possible to predict what kind of financial policies, taxes and interest rates (among other things) will affect our savings between now and then.

But it *is* possible to look at existing successes of ESPs to date and compare them with the potential successes of your own direct investments as described above. I'm sure you'll be surprised at how unspectacular the results of many of the professionally managed funds have been, compared to investors who take the direct approach using conservative shares and buy and sell occasionally to maximise the benefits of semi-regular highs and lows (see Chapter 2). So always:

- Examine the documents provided to you by the fund manager extremely carefully to compare their history against your own successes and the 50-year averages provided by ASIC, shown on page 27.
- Ensure the fund manager discloses their upfront and ongoing fee structure thoroughly, including the 'hidden' brokerage fees that affect each buy and sell share transaction. This affects *all* contributions to the fund, not just your own.
- Ask about performance bonuses that are paid to the fund manager as well as the number of shares in the fund that are

PLANNING EDUCATION COSTS   73

held by each of the board of directors. I don't know about you, but if I ever elect to invest in managed funds, I much prefer to see the directors and fund managers putting their own money where their recommendations are.

- Also ask about the breakdown of the investment portfolio – a nice round pie chart is fast and easy to read for beginners – and if one 'pie-piece' looks chunkier than any others you know instantly where they hope to make most of their 'steady' income. So target your questions to ask about the strategies they'll be using and if they baulk or don't seem to know what they're talking about, then let them see your heels and the dust churned by your wheels as you speed away from them. Because if they don't understand their product properly, how can they expect it to perform as well as they're trying to promise you?

Handy hint: On the upside of ESPs, you can put money away for each nominated child without having to worry about the 66% tax bracket that applies to child investment income that exceeds $417 per financial year. However, it only works to your benefit if the management fees and competence are better than the pounding you suffer from tax.

Warning: There are too many niche investment providers popping up from time to time to risk your hard-earned savings in any kind of financial investment vehicle that is doing dodgy things and very often getting both ASIC and the Tax Office grumpy. So don't take chances with your long-term investments. If you *are* going to choose managed funds, for goodness sake, ONLY go through the big banks, insurance companies and other large financiers that operate right out in the open under the consumer spotlight – and still manage to preserve their long-term reputations at the same time as generating reasonable returns.

7

Primary Schoolers

While your money trees are growing or your managed funds are working away in the background to provide for your kids' long-term education and future, your nippers will be growing up and getting more and more curious about the world. As they reach and progress through primary school, they begin to cover basic maths and maths with money, providing an ideal opportunity for parents to stimulate further interest in family finances and money management. It also provides excellent opportunities for children to learn how theories covered at school can be used and expanded into real-life situations that affect their lives day-to-day. This chapter examines a broad range of strategies to help you achieve this.

For example, if you haven't already started issuing pocket money in exchange for chores then graduation into pre-school or school provides an opportunity to begin the next stage of financial development: the earning and management of pocket money, and the importance of good cash-handling skills.

LESSONS FOR CASH HANDLING AND SHOPPING FOR VALUE

Starting school is a good time to start giving your children cash at the checkouts in shops, then supervising as they hand over the cash and count the change.

Make it easy for six- and seven-year-olds by starting only with cash transactions when you know you'll have easy amounts of money to count – for example, change with no more than one or two coins or notes. Then progress as fast as your child's experience or maturity allows.

Now's also the time to invite your children to keep an eye out for specials on their favourite foods and help choose the best-value groceries – with you scanning the top shelves and them scanning the bottom shelves and calling out the best prices (with you nonchalantly keeping an eye out to make sure they don't miss any).

Handy hint: Get value out of junk mail by putting your children in charge of reading it to find the best prices for your family's favourite grocery brands. Buy in bulk when they spot appropriate bargains and, if you can afford it, share the savings with them 50:50. (See also skill 9 on page 158.)

POCKET MONEY STRATEGIES FOR EARNING, SPENDING AND SAVING

There are three main theories for the distribution of pocket money (aside from not paying it at all), namely:

1. Pocket money paydays – pocket money in exchange for chores and/or good behaviour.
2. All expenses paid with bonuses for extra effort.
3. A combination of the two, comprising a flat allowance with optional bonuses for extra effort or achievements.

If you're a pocket money purist or a financial professional who believes that strategy 1, the nice clean process of paying regular pocket money, is the best method to teach financial principles and reward children for chores AND if you can cross your heart and swear on your favourite bank account that you NEVER have any trouble getting your kids to do their chores week-in week-out without complaint, then please excuse the rest us for a moment while we turn green with envy!

In family wars waged over pocket money, parents are often divided into four main groups:

• Those who pay regular pocket money to their children as a financial learning tool.
• Those who wish they could, but either can't afford it or can't get it working efficiently or harmoniously in their family, so

they involve children and teens in family budgeting with all-expenses paid to the best of their abilities instead.

- Those who do a little of both to suit the individual and changing needs of each child.
- Those who pay pocket money simply because everyone else seems to do it, without properly understanding the options or the lessons they're supposed to be imparting along with it.

At the same time, children fall into two primary ranks across the battlefield: those with skills or natural tendencies to handle pocket money responsibly and those without. And sadly, a lot of unnecessary conflict arises amidst the various family combinations through a lack of cash, confidence, flexibility and/or understanding of the options which are available to them – especially if parents have fallen prey to the misconception that the only way to teach children about finances from an early age is by getting them to earn pocket money through chores.

So it helps to understand the benefits of alternative strategies and the lessons you can teach your children even when pocket money is not a viable option or stops working as a motivator for them to do regular/extra chores.

No strategy is right, wrong or better than any other. They each have benefits and drawbacks. So don't choose the pocket money payday system just because you hear it recommended as standard procedure by many financial advisors. Each family and each child can benefit differently at various stages of their lives depending on which strategy best suits their situation at the time. So benefits can be maximised if parents can be flexible, understand the lessons that can be learned from each strategy, and either use or adapt each strategy to suit their own family's needs, circumstances, characters and stage of financial development. But regardless of which strategy you choose, it's important to remember that:

- some members of the family will always be better in handling money than others;

- paying pocket money in exchange for chores doesn't automatically mean that your child will be financially successful
or develop a good work ethic;
- failing or refusing to pay pocket money does not make you a
bad parent, provided you include the child in family budgeting and understand the benefits and lessons offered by each
of the alternative strategies.

POCKET MONEY: WHOSE IS IT REALLY?
One thing you need to consider before progressing to learn the
three strategies is how you expect your child's pocket money to
be spent. For example, in the case of children under five, who
earn only a dollar or two at a time, you may be content to let
them save or spend the cash with very minimal guidance. For
teenaged children who earn up to $100 per week by working at
home preparing meals and housekeeping to make life easier
for working parents, you may be more likely to encourage
automatic deductions of a negotiated percentage to help save for
their first cars, investments, land deposits or rental bonds for
when they move out. While for teenagers with part-time or full-
time jobs, you may expect them to begin contributions toward
household expenses such as power and water at the same time
as largely supporting themselves.

So in considering each of the following strategies and
adapting them to suit your own situation and ages of children, it will help to remain flexible to the various degrees to
which your offspring will be expected to pay for their own
'needs', such as clothes, meals, haircuts, power and transport
as well as their 'wants', such as fashion accessories, sporting
costs, club memberships, movies, and other entertainment.

STRATEGY 1: POCKET MONEY PAYDAYS (PMPDS)
Parents who implement pocket money paydays for their
children often get the best value for their money by imparting
sound financial values at the same time as linking the payment
of a set amount of weekly pocket money to the completion of

seven days worth of daily chores. But to remain successful with this strategy, parents need to be organised, adept with routine, reliably make payments on time and be firm in ensuring that all chores are done on time and to a set minimum standard each week or fortnight.

Children also need to be co-operative and parents need to have sufficient flexibility in their family budgets to enable payment of unexpected bonuses as rewards for additional efforts. Some families even keep job sheets (usually on the fridge or bedroom doors), which are much like the ones you'd find in a tradesman's toolbox to help keep track of which jobs are completed and due for payment at the end of the week.

Parents best suited to this strategy have room in their budgets to make regular pocket money payments as well as the time or patience needed each day to motivate and re-motivate children into completing chores that haven't been done or done properly. (If you let them do nothing and fall into a pattern of receiving less and less pocket money as punishment, then the system can fall down completely.) Therefore regular pocket money paydays are best suited to families where the income earners are either full-time employees, fixed-income pensioners with low debts, or successful self-employed people who no longer have to work long hours each day.

Low-income earners, casual employees, piece workers and seasonal workers are more likely to struggle with the financial strain of regular pocket money paydays, so increasing the non-monetary rewards for chores while paying a smaller allowance will often help. Trimming back on treats from weekly groceries and paying the cash-value to hard-working children instead (as a sanity allowance) will also provide mature children and teenagers with the choice of either purchasing the treats for themselves or saving the cash for something that's more important to them. (See What is a sanity allowance? on page 133.)

Very busy parents who work long hours may also struggle with the strategy of regular pocket money paydays. Not because

of the strain on the budget, but because time becomes u.
'expensive ingredient' for staying on top of rewarding efforts. So
reserving the biggest chores for the weekend when everyone in
the family can pitch in for half a day (or perhaps two part-
evenings per week) can provide a happy compromise for the
whole family provided that you can chill out enough to put up
with the mess in the meantime. Teenagers with heavy
homework schedules or hectic extra-curricular activities may
prefer performing chores in lump-sessions.

BIGGEST BENEFITS TO THE POCKET-MONEY PAYDAY STRATEGY

- The good habits that result from doing household chores
  regularly, receiving money regularly and then figuring out
  what to do with it – all extremely valuable in adult life.
- Some parents enjoy the prospect of having less hassle
  because they can hand out money once a week and let the
  kids cope with the consequences when they run out.
  Warning: this point can have its own downside if you have
  decided the pocket money you give your under-16-year-olds
  should be used for feeding themselves while away from
  home and paying for transport or clothing – and they're not
  using it for that. As a parent, it's *your* responsibility to ensure
  the basic needs of minors are met, so coming to their rescue
  when they fail can risk rewarding negative behaviour.
- From a budgeting perspective, it helps parents to have a
  firm idea how much they're going to pay out in pocket
  money expenses each week, and if the kids slack off and
  don't earn it, the parents can have budgeting strategies
  in place to effectively spend/reserve it elsewhere. (For
  example, 'parking' the spare cash, no matter how small, in
  either a credit card or a mortgage offset account attached to
  the family home loan – in both cases to minimise interest
  charges and work to the benefit of the family budget at the
  same time as keeping the cash handy until the child *does*
  earn it.)

BIGGEST DOWNSIDES TO THE POCKET MONEY PAYDAY STRATEGY

- Parents need to be diligent in ensuring that time consumed by paperwork, supervision of chores and/or disciplinary action does not eat into the quality time they normally spend with their children.
- Kids with regular pocket money can become blasé about their chores or responsibilities – especially if they already live comfortably or have no financial goals. They could think, 'Why clean my room this week? There's always next week . . .' Degenerative cycles of laziness can begin unless parents remain diligent about supervision of chores or impose penalties for failure to do them properly. Restricting time with friends, computer games or TV are good options for this, and some parents also deduct money from future pocket money, but be particularly careful not to take too much or you can impart a feeling of hopelessness.
- Children can also risk learning that if a job's not worth being paid for, then it's not worth doing. But as we all know, household chores as well as volunteer work later in life must be done without pay so it's important that even children who receive pocket money every week have at least one or two non-paid chores that must be done regularly – no matter what – or else temporarily lose their rights to privileges until they've fulfilled their responsibilities to the family.
- Kids may not agree with how much you feel their labour is worth – 'But Muuum, one lousy dollar for having to make my bed for the whole week? That's slave labour! I can't even buy a packet of chips! And by the way, have you seen the mess I make? Mannn, I need two bucks a day at least!' In this case, negotiation for higher pay in exchange for higher reliability from the child may help you.
- Kids may resent parental influence over what they are allowed to buy with the money they've worked hard to earn – 'But Daaad, your boss doesn't stop *you* from buying junk

food or action computer games!' Respond by discussing the responsibilities that come with money and possibly revise your expectations of how much pocket money will be earned and what proportion of it is expected to be saved and/or spent.

A common challenge for all pocket money strategies: It's important to remember that children should have at least small amounts of money in their wallets nearly all of the time, regardless of whether their parents implement a pocket money payday or not.

STRATEGY 2: ALL-EXPENSES-PAID (AEP) (PLUS OPTIONAL BONUSES)

At the opposite end of the playing field, we have the equally dedicated parents who pay all their children's living expenses, restricting small regular treats to those purchased among the weekly groceries – but only as rewards for good behaviour. Valuable treats are left for birthdays, Christmas and the other moments they can afford them – and only then if the kids have behaved really well for an extended length of time. Optional bonuses can then become available as a reward for extra effort (on top of household chores that must be done) and these can be either cash or non-monetary rewards.

Parents on this side of the pocket money battlefield are usually strict budgeters, whether it's by choice or forced upon them by economic circumstances.

BIGGEST BENEFITS TO THE ALL-EXPENSES-PAID (AEP) STRATEGY

- Children gain a strong appreciation for money and treats because they're relatively rare.
- Children gain money management skills for bigger lump-sum payments which are paid infrequently.
- The requirement of children to give change back to parents

for purchases provides them with practice at reporting expenses to employers and imparts additional confidence in being trusted regularly with cash assets of value to the whole family. When strict budgets are forced upon a family, the AEP method also generates a greater appreciation for the impact of individual expenses on the rest of the family, a desire to earn extra cash on their own (outside of the family) and a greater desire to contribute back to the family as soon as their own needs have been met and exceeded (with the exception of naturally generous children, of course, who behave as they do, no matter which 'team' they're from).

- Kids learn survival strategies to make money stretch longer through difficult times.
- Since transactions in and out of wallets are greatly reduced for AEP children, it can be easier for them to remember how much they and each of their siblings have (roughly at least) in their wallets at any time.
- Parents who implement the AEP strategy usually have an easier time insisting on good behavior from bored youngsters during trips to the shopping centre, because the youngsters know that the treats they 'earn' all week/fortnight for good behaviour can be lost, deferred or greatly reduced at the last minute if they fail to make it all the way through the checkout and out to the car without a tantrum.
- Parents who use the AEP strategy can also enjoy the prospect of having less hassle keeping track of jobs, fewer arguments over whether chores were done well enough to be paid, and less time consumed in having to prepare 'pay-packets' each week at the same time.
- From a budgeting perspective, the AEP strategy also helps to ensure that every coin in the family works as hard as possible in minimising debt and interest expenses until it's needed, without sitting around 'semi-uselessly' in children's wallets and moneyboxes. This is especially true if large portions of your child's pocket money is intended for them to buy their

own clothes or monthly public transport tickets. With AEP these can be purchased on your credit card to maximise point accrual for the family. Provided the children are involved in the household budgeting, receive as many non-monetary rewards as possible for their efforts and still have the option of working harder to earn cash bonuses, the AEP method can actually generate greater savings which can also be passed on to children by way of lifestyle improvements and family luxuries.

BIGGEST DOWNSIDES TO THE ALL-EXPENSES-PAID STRATEGY (AEP)

- Kids without regular pocket money still have cash in their wallets, but it has to be budgeted much more carefully, so their opportunities for learning cash-transaction skills may be reduced unless they're provided with additional opportunities. One way of doing this is by involving mature children with the shopping more often, sending them to the freezer, bread or pet food aisles to select the best-value items. Teens can even be sent to one end of the supermarket with a trolley while you start at the opposite end, and then shop until you meet in the middle or back at the checkouts (and get finished faster). Make sure you choose age-appropriate assignments for safety purposes and never lose sight of young children! Littlies don't have to miss out either. They can be placed in line at cinemas to buy yummies with cash while you either stand behind them, or for upper primary schoolers, stand back and watch from a safe distance. Kids without regular pocket money still gain cash handling skills at the school tuckshop, but parents have to be a little more diligent about receiving change back into the 'tuckshop cash reserve' at home or in the car.
- When a child enters high school the AEP method doesn't usually work as well, since teenagers require cash funds in their wallet for safety purposes. At this point a switch to a pocket money or allowance-based system can be helpful.

- It can be easy for parents to forget to reward well-behaved children with generous bonuses when the family can afford it. Try to budget to achieve this at least twice a year (making sure to pay it during a period of good behaviour, of course!). To this end, it will help to remember what you were like as a child at the same age and try to pass on money as if you were passing the cash back through time to yourself – remembering to at least double or triple the amount involved to compensate for inflation!

- Kids can feel hard done by when they realise that other kids at school receive regular pocket money. Avoid this by explaining the different methodologies as soon as your child is old enough to come home and ask why they aren't getting any pocket money, when all their mates seem to get pocket money for nothing. You can also help them choose for themselves which way they want to go from now on, seeing as they've been responsible in bringing the new proposal to you, by working out how much they currently get in 'real value' by having all their expenses paid for them. Then work out the same situation for them assuming they have to do EXTRA chores regularly without fail in order to get money and then have to pay for everything themselves. Or it could be time to negotiate the compromise of all expenses paid, plus a small allowance for regular extra efforts. But with the proviso, of course, that no matter which new method they choose – small allowance or full-rate pocket money – there's no coming back for safe sanctuary. Or else they'll miss the lesson about financial consequences and quickly learn that they can come back to bludge off Mum and Dad whenever they blow their own money.

Did you know?

Some of my most treasured childhood memories include the rare days that my father would be able to afford to give us pocket money – usually only once or twice a year – and usually after working months of really long hours. He'd call us all in, hiding his hands behind his back, then a sly smile would slide across his face and he'd make us report how good we'd been before presenting each of us with a $20, $50 or $100 note, which to us, was akin to $100 to $500 nowadays! How rich we felt! How proud of him we were! And how very, very careful we each were to ensure that we didn't waste a cent!

STRATEGY 3: COMPROMISE WITH A FLAT ALLOWANCE PLUS BONUSES

This strategy is a flexible combination of pocket money paydays and the bonuses from the all-expenses-paid strategy. It works by assigning a small number of chores that must be done regularly in order to receive the flat allowance. There is also a choice of additional chores that can be done – like overtime in the workplace – in order to earn extra cash. And just like overtime that's offered to (or forced upon) parents in the workplace, the chores can be offered to or required of children from time to time, depending on urgency to the family. For example, an upcoming party or unexpected sleepover from a relative may require 'all-hands-on-deck' to prepare for the occasion, with extra work paid for accordingly.

ON THE SUBJECT OF PAYING BONUSES TO CHILDREN

Allowing children to earn money as rewards for attempting or improving their skills at their chores, or through quiz prizes that make a game of testing knowledge or skills, can help to teach them about responsibility, reward for effort, value of denominations, and it makes the youngsters feel more important and trusted enough to have money 'like a grown up', even if the true face value of the money is negligible.

How you guide children to spend their pocket money provides valuable opportunities to introduce concepts of generosity, value-for-money and short-term investment.

Warning: Beware of providing 'bonus' payments to children before they're able to understand why they're receiving the extra cash, because the cheeky little tikes can sometimes become expert at expecting or wheedling a reward out of you without having to provide any reasonable effort or they can expect a cash bonus every time they help. Irregular pocket money from grandparents falls into this category too, so rather than refusing or avoiding such situations, I've found it best to enforce one of my favourite fun rules for success – ***Rule 4: Quick cash is loathe to last.*** This means that if cash comes to you unexpectedly, then it's likely to leave just as quickly unless you make it hang around for the long term by either adding it to savings to help turn your distant dreams into goals achieved, or using it to pay off debts and help you to start the rest of your life afresh.

Note: Some parents may be wondering why I mention paying off debts to start your life afresh in a book about finances for kids, since you'd hardly expect teenagers to graduate from a free secondary education into adult life with debts already hanging over their heads. But the sad truth is that many teenagers do indeed overspend on their clothes, furniture, mobile phone, entertainment expenses and owe debts to their friends, step-parents or grandparents – sometimes without their parents' prior knowledge or consent! (Teenagers who participate in overseas student exchange programs often have debts to their parents to pay off as well.)

ON THE SUBJECT OF CASH IN LIEU OF PRESENTS

Very young children have no concept of either pressies or money. They're much more likely to play with the wrapping paper, because that's the bit that looks nice when they get it. You can't feel insulted because they don't pay any attention to the gift inside it, you just have to take your time and help them learn how to enjoy the gift.

And it's the same at the next stage of 'premature gift development'. If your child opens their pressies to find an absence of cool socks, shirts or jumpers with their favourite characters stenciled in bright colours all over them and instead holds up money or gift vouchers as if it were somebody's dirty undies, then you need to sit down for a crash course in excitement-packed brainstorming, visualisation and goalsetting.

'Gee, wow!' you'll have to exclaim excitedly. 'Let's make a list of all the cool things you can buy (or save up for) and then we can go shopping!'

ON THE SUBJECT OF CASH IN LIEU OF PARTIES

As soon as children start to figure out what money is all about, it can be extremely interesting and valuable to them as a life experience to work out roughly how much their next birthday party would cost (at least six months in advance) and offer them two options:

1. A full-scale birthday party with friends, where they often get many little presents, a half day of fun and lots of mess to clean up.
2. A small-scale dinner with close family where the child chooses their favourite meal at home or a restaurant, plus one daytrip to toy stores where they can buy absolutely anything and everything they want up to the total value of what you would have spent on option 1 anyway.

But there are a few provisos:

- In order for children to make a healthy, informed decision, they have to have at least one really amazing birthday party with friends in their toybox of experience already.
- It has to stay 'business as usual' in being allowed to have friends over to play on the weekends at the same rate that they do every other month of the year.

- They must be allowed to change their minds any time up to their birthday (on the understanding that if you don't get a fortnight's notice to allow time for bookings and invitations, they'll probably have to wait an extra week or three to get their party).
- All purchases must get final approval from a parent before heading to the checkouts to ensure the little eager beaver isn't getting ripped off or buying junk that will break 10 seconds after being opened, making sure to explain these concepts to help your financially developing child compare prices, quality and warranty while shopping. However, for very low value items (e.g. under $10, which actually seems like an awful lot to young children), it can very often be a good lesson for them to have their hard-earned junk purchases fail to last after getting them home, so they are more careful next time. When it comes time for them to buy their first car, you'll want the concept of value and quality firmly understood, or else they risk falling prey to lemons or hot-rods that attract repair bills or police attention!
- They can't do it two years in a row.

Just imagine it! For a child or teenager, being taken into a toy, book or games superstore and allowed to spend anywhere between $100 and $500 in one day (depending on how much you usually spend on their parties) is like giving $50,000 to $100,000 to an adult and sending them into a superstore of *their* choice. It's a life experience we all dream of – and one that's only affordable in a family budget while the child's concept of 'extravagant' is still less than the quarterly power bill.

They'll also be getting a crash course in value-for-money, because the child is suddenly faced with a vast range of all their desires in one place, able to afford more than one high-quality item (possibly for the first time ever), while having the most money they've ever imagined – and *still* having to make difficult choices while filling their arms or trolley with 'treasure'.

For five- to ten-year-olds (especially), the idea of having so much to choose from presents them with opportunity overload. So combining youthful excitement with the possibility of being able to spend their budget over a 'birthday week' instead of a single day can provide you with an extra opportunity to reinforce the value of patience in waiting to get exactly what they want, rather than buying at the first opportunity or buying things just for the sake of buying them. For a child with money in their pockets, this challenge can actually make them *want* to hold off buying something until they can buy exactly what they desire.

ON THE SUBJECT OF DOLLAR-FOR-DOLLAR DEALS

Often mature children and teenagers can be enticed to save or work harder by offering them dollar-for-dollar savings. For example: 'Hey, sweetie! You know that computer game you're saving up for? Well, if you can cut back on your cash expenses in order to save $5 per week from your pocket money, I'll give you a $5 bonus to add to your savings account! And if you can save $6, I'll give you a $6 bonus. $10 for $10, and so on. Is it a deal?'

At least that's the theory. Personally, I haven't had much luck with it unless I mention it in a way that my children end up proposing it back to me as if it was their idea. Otherwise, they try haggling for a $2 for $1 deal! But every child is different, so it could be worth trying for your children.

CHORES WITHOUT REWARDS

In our house, we have a small number of chores that each child must perform regularly without any expectation of payment. These chores must be done before the kids can be paid for any other cash-earning chores and failure to do them results in 'lifestyle penalties' such as no TV, no computer games, no phone calls to friends or no bike riding.

This is mainly to guard against the idea that a job is only worth doing if you're paid for it, but we've also found it helps emphasise the difference between minimum expectations and rewards for extra efforts as well as ensuring that our children understand that lifestyle luxuries are a privilege, not a right.

We also aim for maximum flexibility with almost unlimited potential for earning pocket money. For example, if the kids want to work to earn pocket money, even when we've run out of chores, we'll let them start a new garden, paint a fence, catalogue our videos, reorganise our library or help out a relative, to provide 'overtime' opportunities that also benefit the whole family.

But each child and each family is different and these differences change as each child matures so I've provided the following two lists of suggestions to help you design a flexible program to suit yourselves:

Choose 1 to 5 mandatory tasks
(that pay either no, or a minimum rate of pocket money.)

- Make your own bed
- Feed the pets
- Tidy your own room
- Water the garden
- Unstack/restack dishwasher
- Take out rubbish
- Help fetch groceries from car
- Finish homework on time
- Check the mailbox
- Help with the mowing
- Help pack away groceries
- Tidy shoes at front door

Extra chores for bonus pocket money
(*Handy hint:* Assign $1 to $10 per chore, depending on how hard they are and write them out in order so your child can see at a glance what each is worth.)

- Tidy bathroom
- Fill washing machine
- Fill toilet roll holders
- Sweep/mop patios
- Wash front door
- Hose BBQ table
- Wipe coffee tables
- Wash bath tub
- Scrub laundry tub
- Wipe fingerprints off power points and door handles
- Sweep kitchen/rumpus/ family room
- Organise saucepan or plastic container cupboards
- Sweep ceiling corners inside or gutters outside for cobwebs

- Tidy cutlery drawer
- Finish homework before it's due
- Scrub shower tiles
- Shake out floor mats
- Wipe bathroom mirrors
- Wash dog/car/bikes/mower
- Sweep floor cornices for dust
- Tidy videos and DVDs
- Mop toilet floor
- Get bugs out of letterbox
- Vacuum bedroom/lounge
- Vacuum car

Handy hint: Before assigning pocket money and tasks to children, spend one whole day having a massive spring clean with the whole family. All hands on deck, as we call it. That way, you can start your new pocket-money program with a thoroughly clean house, which is always much less intimidating for young children to keep clean with smaller regular efforts. And in the process of spring cleaning, attack each room one-by-one, make a list of all the little tasks it takes to get back on top of things and magnet it to the fridge so children always have access to a much wider choice of 'bonus chores' to do whenever they wish to earn additional pocket money.

NON-MONETARY REWARDS

These can be good for providing extra rewards for children who deserve them, even when family budgets are too stretched to pay bonus pocket money. Here are some of our favourites, but don't forget to add your family favourites to the list too:

- A goal-setting trip to the local toystore, bookshop, bike shop or clothes store;
- A sleep-over with friends;
- Watch TV;
- Time playing computer games;
- Cash in loyalty points on your credit cards for music, book or game gift vouchers;
- Visit the public library where the latest computer games and books are available;

- Download a new freeware computer game or two;
- A trip to the park or bike track;
- A gift voucher to get out of chores for one day/week of the child's choice.

LOW-COST REWARDS

These can help the family budget stretch a little further at the same time as teaching children about value-for-money fun. Again, here are some of our favourites. Don't forget to brain-storm a few extras with your own children.

- Hire a DVD, video or computer game from the local video shop;
- Spend time on the Internet to search for computer game hints and cheat-codes;
- Play free computer games online (check the links on my website, www.anitabell.com);
- Make phone-calls to friends;
- Go tenpin bowling;
- Play mini-golf or hire a tennis court;
- Go see a movie at the cinema;
- Buy new accessories for push-bikes;
- $5 to $10 savings bonus.

HOW MUCH POCKET MONEY?

A recent Australian survey of 400 children aged between 8 and 12 found that that the average pocket money paid to them is $4.90 per week, and that:

- 38% receive less than $5 per week;
- 56% get between $5 and $10;
- 6% earn $10 or more.

Every family seems to have a different view on this one, depending on their budget, the pocket money strategy they use and each child's level of maturity, work ethic and money-handling skills. Here are a handful of the most popular methods I've come across:

- **Price-your-age**: $1 for each year of the child's life. For example a five-year-old gets $5 a week, an eight-year-old gets $8 a week, while a 16 year old gets . . . you can guess.
- **As-needs-be**: Work out how much the child needs each week for whatever you've decided they are to pay for with their pocket money, then add a percentage between 10% and 20% to allow for savings.
- **Piecework**: Each chore is assigned a pocket money value and each child is paid for each job completed. (But be careful to ensure equal opportunity between children of different ages so that cunning children don't hog the more valuable chores. For example, kids who are too young to mow the lawn won't see the justice of doing three or four smaller or more time-consuming jobs to earn the same money.
- **Cyber-credits**: This method relies on points being kept in cyberspace – your computer or on a scoreboard on the fridge – with points added for good behaviour and/or chores completed. It also involves deducting points for each episode of bad behaviour and/or chores avoided. Totals are taken each week or month and the child can either purchase an item of their choice (on your credit card so you also get loyalty bonus points), or they can save the points for the next month in order to buy something more valuable.

> **Warning:** Some parents 'charge' their children for breakages of glasses or plates, which can be a helpful and cost-effective punishment for kids who are notoriously reckless. But it won't help children who are genuinely or innocently clumsy. In fact if it makes them feel even worse about themselves to be charged every time they stumble and break things, then you could easily undermine the concept of pocket money by punishing kids for events that are beyond their control. Sure, it happens in real life. Flat tyres, dirty fuel, car accidents and sporting injuries are all costly misadventures for adults which fall into the same kind of 'bad-luck' basket as broken crockery

for children. But as one of my favourite baby bibs says: *Spit happens. Live with it.* So for children who break things only rarely, the shock of the accident and the guilt in breaking something they've just enjoyed using can be punishment enough.

PERCENTAGE FOR SAVINGS

Australian children are remarkably good at saving their pocket money, with children under eight years old often banking approximately 66 cents for every dollar received, while 8- to 12-year-olds typically bank half of their pocket money.

Some children save up 100% of their pocket money in a bank account and then withdraw as much as they need as soon as they've stashed away enough to purchase the item they've been slaving to save for. Others don't save anything. And still others save their money into piggy banks and money socks in secret quantities known only to them (and parents who discover their hiding places!).

Finding a healthy balance for your own child usually means encouraging them to save no less than $1 and no more than $9 in every $10 earned. Since it's often impractical and frustrating for children who receive less than $10 to muck around with the banking or spending of negligible small change, it's much better for them to save it up in a piggy bank, secret safe or money sock before 'budgeting' their money into savings and expenses – where savings can also be split into 'long-term savings' and 'savings for special goals', even if they're managed inside the one bank account by using hand-written notes recording balances glued or pencilled into the passbook.

PERCENTAGE FOR EXPENDITURE

The survey also revealed the spending habits of 8- to 12-year-old children, with:

- 39% of youngsters spending pocket money on treat-style foods;

- 25% either saving up or spending immediately on toys;
- 22% with their hearts and wallets aimed at CDs or computer games;
- 20% spending their money on clothes.

However, it's important not to leap to the conclusion that most children waste their money on junk food, since many under-12s aren't permitted to have junk food unless they work and pay for it themselves. At the other end of the scale, many under-12s have the majority of their most expensive desires in music, clothes, books, toys and computer games met by gifts for birthdays, Easter and Christmas, so there's less need for them to purchase anything except new releases in-between times.

VALUE FOR EXPENDITURE

As a fun and insightful exercise to measure if your child has been spending wisely, try doing the following quick and easy exercises with them.

1. Once a year – or once every month or quarter if it suits you better – sit down with your children and work out how much pocket money they've earned during the previous period.
2. Make a list of the approximate cost of everything they've purchased.
3. Work out an approximation of how much has slipped through their fingers as expenditure on things they've eaten, broken or used in entertainment that doesn't have a resale value (e.g. going to theme parks, game parlours or movies).
4. Add a column beside their list of purchases and list the approximate second-hand values if they sold the items at a garage sale, Cash Converters or through eBay.
5. Add these new items and their second-hand values to a running total of each child's belongings and explain this as being their 'net asset value' – the amount considered to be a measure of their wealth after all debts like loans and IOUs have been deducted. Remember that it's common and

understandable for a certain 'sanity allowance' portion of their pocket money to be spent regularly on personal treats and entertainment. (See also page 133.)

6. Discuss the value of your child's 'net asset wealth' and their total wealth (including cash reserves in bank account savings, piggy-bank coins and money still sitting in their wallet).

7. Use the opportunity to ask if they would like to revise their savings goals, perhaps putting more aside for long-term savings as well as short-term savings for special goals.

8. Allow your children to see you doing the same exercise for the household budget at least twice a year so they can see how the principles of micro-budgets like theirs are used in a similar method for family budgets – just with larger amounts of money. And at the same time, explain how good family budgets and pocket-money budgets work on the same principles (generally speaking) as macro-budgets used for major national and international companies.

QUASI-PAY PACKETS FOR VOLUNTEER WORK

Understanding first that volunteer work is meant to be unpaid while encouraging a healthy work ethic and accruing job skills, there can be benefits in paying pocket money or cash bonuses to children as an extra unexpected reward out of your own pocket when they're helping you with:

• fundraising efforts for their sports club, scouts, school, daycare centre or local kindergarten (even if they no longer go there, but younger siblings do);

• profit-sharing from garage sales, weekend markets or eBay sales that they help you with;

• volunteer work at old folk's homes, community centres or resource centres for physically disabled children (especially on craft days, market days or outings on bus trips).

And while payment might not always be appropriate, the following endeavours can also help to provide your child with more money-handling skills:

- readathons
- Jump Rope for Heart
- pie drives
- walkathons

- World's Greatest Shave
- selling chocolates
- spellathons
- 40 Hour Famine

Handy hints: Even though your child won't be paid by the organisation they volunteer for, they will often be provided with a certificate of participation/appreciation afterwards. This always looks impressive on a résumé for a school leaver and can help demonstrate and provide evidence of team skills, a healthy community-mindedness and specific job skills such as cash-handling, communication skills or care of the elderly or disabled.

ON THE SUBJECT OF BORROWING MONEY BACK FROM YOUR KIDS

Caught short of cash over the weekend? Then don't rush straight to a hole in the wall to get more. First try giving your kids an opportunity to loan you any pocket money they might have at home. They'll feel responsible for helping out the family in a pinch, you could pay them interest for their trouble and they'll witness their parents making dollars stretch resourcefully without using credit cards and bank accounts.

8

High School and the Teen Years

This chapter provides an overview of the most popular topics requested of me from high schools. Not surprisingly, it also happens to cover most of the topics that I wish *I'd* been taught at the same stage, including lots about employment issues. But this is a time in life when teenagers are learning a lot, starting to put it into practice and becoming more self-sufficient, so before we begin, you need to make sure your teenager is slick with all the topics we've already covered. Then we need to get into the right headspace together.

GETTING INTO THE RIGHT HEADSPACE
Senior high students (and junior high students who are mature-minded enough to be holding down casual or part-time jobs while still attending school) are young adults with a universe of new challenges. Whenever I refer to a teenager I also mean mature-minded children wherever the topic may also apply to them.

Now is the time to appreciate teenagers' natural talents of observation and mimicry. They've been watching you – a lot like covert experts in surveillance – since they were fang-high to the family rottweiler. But by their teen years, they may have switched off these talents and be coasting on a cloud of partial knowledge, having assumed they've figured out why adults do as they do and how they can get by when it's their turn to be in charge of their lives.

Take credit cards, for example. A financially literate adult will reach for their credit card only when they know they're able to pay it off completely by the end of the month, thus avoiding use of any EFTPOS card which has bank fees. Or they may have the inner strength and resolve to defer the purchase until it can be better afforded. Or they may walk down the street to the bank and withdraw the cash from an account manually. But a financially illiterate teenager – who has used observational skills over the years to build a basic knowledge of credit cards and how to 'hand over the plastic' whenever there are insufficient funds in their wallet – could view the adult's alternative choices as inefficient mucking around. (The roles could easily be reversed, though, with the adult being less financially literate than the teenager.)

So from here on, I suggest that whenever you discuss financial products or services with your teenagers and mature-minded children, you do so with a respect for their intelligence and natural observational skills by asking if they can think of any alternatives and then discussing the pros and cons of each option rationally.

And now that we're all in the right headspace, I'm tempted to say, 'Pull up a couple of armchairs and let's go through the rest of this book together'. But honestly, I think you'll all get a lot more out of the next few chapters if you take turns reading them, and then at the end compare notes with your family, friends or teachers before making it happen. So this chapter has been written for both adults and teenagers.

HOBBY JOBS

By the time your child is in high school they may be starting to show interest in earning money beyond their pocket money. Here are a few options for bringing in extra cash:

Newspaper delivery Service to 250 homes twice a week earns about $150 per month, but varies from state to state, so contact your local newsagent for details. The money isn't much considering the work involved, but the work ethic needed is good and delivering in your local area means there's lots of exercise without huge distances to pick up or deliver.

Letterbox distribution for local or family businesses Kids can try offering a flat-fee to distribute brochures and pamphlets for local business owners. Business owners usually pay $20 to $40 for delivery of 250 pamphlets, or $50 to $250 for 1000 to 3000 pamphlets, but either way, they have to know they can trust you to get the leaflets into the hands of potential clients without dumping them in the nearest rubbish bin as soon as you walk around the corner. That can be hard work for kids, but you can make it worthwhile and safer by paying them to take your dog for a walk at the same time, provided your dog isn't the type to make mischief!

Babysitting 14- to 18-year-olds can earn between $5 and $20 per hour, depending on their age, the number and ages of children to be cared for, the time of day as well as the location (whether it's done at your home or the home of the babysittees). If in doubt about what to charge, ring your local babysitting service to ask what they charge for their professional services, and then suggest that your children offer a 20% to 50% discount, depending on how desperate they are and the total amount of money involved. It's best to start by looking after neighbours' and nearby friends' children, so a parent is only a few doors away in case of an emergency, and it's an excellent idea for anyone planning to babysit to attend a First Aid course first.

Tutoring If your child has high grades in a particular subject they could tutor younger children. Again, rates charged will depend on their age and the age of the child being tutored.

Money from homework Well-written assignments on non-fiction local topics can form the basis of interesting articles for local newspapers and magazines. Use feedback from teachers' remarks as free advice for editing. Take digital photographs to support the story and email (or post) them to your local newspaper – calling first to make sure they're interested. Payment rates vary depending on word count, and the most easily sold stories are usually between 100 and 500 words, earning anything from $50 to $450, with humourous anecdotes earning $50 to $250! You can borrow a library copy of *The Australian Writers' Marketplace* for details of more newspapers, magazines and publishers who accept unsolicited articles and stories (unsolicited = work that hasn't been requested).

Lucrative hobbies Growing plants, raising quality breeding pets, making jewellery, clay plant pots, baby clothes, special-occasion cakes or mass-producing anything that your teenager has received good grades for learning to do in manual arts classes not only occupies busy minds and hands with enjoyable pastimes, but can also earn $200 to $2000 a year, depending on how much they produce and sell at markets, garage sales and through networks of friends and relatives.

TV extras and commercial advertising Register with your local talent agency for availability as an extra in TV commercials or background shots for movies. While you're at it, you may like to register the whole family! You don't have to be skinny and gorgeous – often the more 'normal' the better. Half a day's work can earn each of you $200 to $500 for sitting around, even if it turns out they don't need you!

Furniture restoration Don't laugh! Some kids are really talented at this. Start small by raiding the garages at your parents' and grandparents' homes for belongings that haven't been used in centuries, then clean them up, sand them down, paint them and sell them for a profit through no-cost newspaper ads, local second-hand stores or eBay. Old bar fridges are excellent fun for artistic kids to restore – turn them into real pieces of art! Profits for hand-renovated *objets d'art* can often range between $20 to $300 per piece.

Junior garage sale Ask your child to clear out all their old toys, clothes, books and computer games. Selling them through eBay, garage sales or free newspaper ads can give them helpful experience at running a 'shop', especially if they're old enough to help you with pricing, security guard duties and cash handling during the sale.

Handy hint: Selling hotdogs (provided it's okay in your council district) and cold drinks at your garage sale can often double your earnings for the day.

Weekend carwashes With parental supervision, kids can run weekend car-washing enterprises, making sure that in times of drought, they use buckets, rather than leaving hoses running. Try doing this at home in the driveway or down at your local service station, hardware store or car sales yard (where people leave their cars while test-driving).

Local bike shop These often offer volunteer positions after school and during holidays for children – no pay, but the right to discounts on bikes and bike parts while learning how bikes work and how to fix them.

See pages 106–7 for a list of 'unskilled' jobs suitable for teenagers, some of which also employ juniors and part-timers.

FIRST TAXES FOR CHILDREN

If your child starts earning income from 'professionalising' one of the hobby jobs mentioned above, it's important for them to learn how the government treats such income. Cash income can usually be treated as non-taxable hobby income, just as it would be for an adult – so there will be no need to collect or pay an extra 10% GST (Goods and Services Tax) to the Tax Office. But if your child earns and banks income as if it were adult income, then the Tax Office *may* decide that income tax at adult rates is payable. (See tax scales on page 166.) Rules for such decisions are extremely complicated and fuzzy, though, often depending on what exactly your child does in order to earn the money, how often they earn it and how much effort is involved compared to their profit margins (among other things), so always consult your family's accountant if your child earns more than $417 per financial year from any kind of self-operated micro-business. (See also On the subject of hobbies and business paperwork, page 173.) Adult tax rates will apply if your child earns income as if they were operating a business and tries to claim tax deductions for expenses.

If they earn between $2000 and $20,000 per financial year, it's possible to achieve tax and cash-flow benefits by registering with the Australian Tax Office for an Australian Business

Number (ABN), with the option to register for GST purposes. *Note:* If you register for an ABN, then you don't necessarily have to register for GST provided that your income is under $50,000 a year. But if you register for GST, you must also register for an ABN. And if you do end up registering for GST at this (usually premature) stage, then your child also has to charge an extra 10% GST for their goods or services, which must be sent to the Tax Office (easier to manage if it's done every quarter) with blank returns that must be lodged each time they stop their businesses to go back to full time study (or de-register by closing their micro-business).

Warning: Micro-money-making ventures that involve gambling – such as raffles, mini-lotto or side-show-alley-style games – are strictly regulated and unlawful unless conducted by registered game operators or registered for fundraising purposes by an approved organization, such as kindergartens, school Parents & Citizens/Friends Associations, sporting clubs and charities. These all have to pay to renew their licences regularly and can have their licences revoked for breaching the official rules of conduct.

ON THE SUBJECT OF TAX AND THE AGE KIDS CAN WORK

The official age from which children can legally begin earning money varies from state to state, so contact the Department of Industrial relations in your state for more information. Duty of care issues also exist for employers to provide suitable supervision and work conditions. It will really come down to when you think your child is mature and responsible enough to manage some part-time work without it adversely affecting their education, social development or your family life.

However, if children are under 18 years of age, still full-time students and they're going to earn more than $417 per year, they'll need to be able to show that the work is age-appropriate and completed on a day-to-day basis by maintaining tax records (for seven years after the work is done) in the form of payslips, timesheets and/or dated and signed diary entries which show how many hours they worked.

Even if your child is going to earn less than $417 for the financial year, make sure they still fill in a tax declaration as soon as they start work as an extra indication to the Tax Office that they're working in an official capacity. It can save hassles later if they begin to earn more than $417 for that financial year or soon after.

If your child has a choice between receiving payment for their work by cheque, cash or a direct bank deposit, suggest they choose a bank deposit or cash because:

a. a bank deposit provides evidence of working in an official capacity for tax purposes, despite being a minor;

b. cheque deposits take time to clear and usually result in the deduction of bank fees.

Warning: It's possible that children can overdo it when it comes to working for their first paypackets, particularly when it comes to manual labour. Many boys especially view themselves as indestructible, so it's important to ensure they know the importance of keeping their bodies hydrated, techniques for lifting heavy weights and basic first aid skills. Remind them of the importance of balancing work, rest and play, while prioritising their efforts when necessary to achieve workplace deadlines and personal goals.

JOBS FOR SENIOR HIGH SCHOOL STUDENTS

As a teenager, a part-time job that pays youth wages usually provides your first semi-permanent reliable income. Youth wages are a percentage of full-time adult wages; even though you are very often doing the same work as an adult, there is an assumption that you're not as fast or as efficient when you're young and inexperienced. For example, as a 17-year-old you might get 55% of an adult's wage, depending what job you're doing, while a 19-year-old doing exactly the same job may be entitled to 75 to 80%. This is often fair enough for many young school leavers who have little previous work experience, but it can be unfair on the ones who really do put a lot of effort in and may even work twice as hard and efficiently as an adult. But don't worry too much if you are one of these super-efficient people. If you're that good, your employer will try to keep you at the end of your traineeship, instead of letting you go in order to hire another 'cheap' worker.

For an idea of how much income every job in Australia is roughly entitled to (allowing for a little variation between states) check out the website at www.worksite.actu.asn.au and follow the links from the menu to job-union match to see the rates of pay. Or for a range of samples see the following table, which includes some of the most popular casual and part-time jobs from the retail, building and hospitality industries.

SAMPLES OF 'LOW-SKILLED' AND 'UNSKILLED' JOBS

It's quite common for reliable and hardworking 'low-skilled' or 'unskilled' employees to form the backbone of major companies. Another interesting thing about such jobs is that students and school leavers seeking part-time work while still studying don't necessarily have to wait for vacancies to be advertised before applying. You can often simply walk in, register your interest in applying for a job, hand in a copy of your résumé (containing no originals of certificates), have an on-the-spot interview if you're really lucky or go on a waiting list to be interviewed as soon as the next vacancy arises.

And don't get upset by my use of the terms 'low-skilled' and 'unskilled'. These are official terms used to describe jobs where:
- people applying for the vacancies may have started a course, traineeship or apprenticeship with another course provider or employer, but not yet finished;
- only basic 'employability skills' are required in order to function as a valuable employee. Basic employability skills may vary from industry to industry and workplace to workplace but, generally speaking, they nearly always include:
  - basic literacy skills: reading, writing, conversation, communication;

- o basic numeracy skills: maths, calculator and cash-handling skills;
- o basic computer skills: starting up, shutting down, typing and use of word-processing software;
- o phone skills and personal presentation skills.

These are the kinds of jobs for which companies will often consider hiring a student or recent school leaver. Here is a list of a few suggestions which may help point you in the right direction:

Job	Minimum basic weekly wage (rounded to the nearest $5)	Further studies can be done at:
Pathology aide	$ 485	TAFE
Shop assistant (including fast-food attendant)	$255	Not applicable
Bar/waiting staff (but can't serve alcohol until 18 years old)	$ 465 (up to 40% less if aged 17 to 20)	TAFE (In NSW, the Responsible Service of Alcohol (RSA) TAFE course is compulsory for bar staff)
Actor/performer	$600	TAFE/ university
Animal attendant @ vet/zoo	$450	TAFE/ university
Bank officer	$480	Not applicable

Job	Minimum basic weekly wage (rounded to the nearest $5	Further studies can be done at:
Beautician	$480	TAFE
Cleaner	$515 – dayshift $650 nightshift	Not applicable
Dancer	$570	TAFE/ university
Delivery driver (includes pizza delivery)	$480	Not applicable
Dental assistant	$500	TAFE
Fitness instructor	$480	TAFE/ university
Hairdresser	$190 to $540	Apprenticeship
Journalist	$450	TAFE/ university
Builders' labourer	$540	TAFE
Librarian's assistant	$600	TAFE/ university
Receptionist	$500 but may be less if junior rates apply	TAFE/ receptionist colleges

OTHER OPPORTUNITIES TO MAKE MONEY

Apart from a part-time job, there are numerous ways entre-preneurial students at high school can make a bit of extra cash by using their skills and imaginations:

- The Annual $1000 Crusader Youth Encouragement Award for readers of my *Kirby's Crusader* series who would love an opportunity to set their dream careers in motion, but are challenged by the socio-economic circumstances of their family. Details are on my website at anitabell.com.
- The Nescafé Big Break Competition is held annually and gives 16- to 24-year-olds in Australia and New Zealand the chance to win a cash kick-start to help get their career or innovative business idea off the ground. Details are on their website at www.nescafebigbreak.com.
- State- and council-sponsored youth citizens awards are held annually in all states and in many cities and shires around Australia. Prizes vary from $500 to $250,000 and cover a wide range of interests from creative arts to business, sports, community awards and young achiever awards, often including prize money, trophies, scholarships or interstate trips. For more info, contact your local council or see websites:
  - www.thesource.gov.au/involve/youth_awards.asp
  - www.awardsaustralia.com/YAA.html
  - www.futureleaders.com.au.
- Business innovation grants are available to varying degrees in each city, state and region through your local council office. For example:
  - The *Yellow Pages* Business Ideas Grants with prize pool up to $200,000. See www.about.sensis.com.au/big/
  - Qantas youth awards: www.qantas.com.au/info/about/community/sharingTheSpirit
  - For a fairly comprehensive A to Z listing of awards and opportunities specific to music, arts, writing, film and cartooning for young people, see the Australian Government Youth Initiative (Commonwealth Department of Family and Community Sevice) website: www.thesource.gov.au/livingchoices.

ON THE SUBJECT OF DROPPING OUT OF SCHOOL EARLY

Don't kid yourself. Unless you have a full-time job with an employer who's supportive of you then the chances of getting *and keeping* a job for more than the first six months after dropping out of school are just a little better than 50%. Statistics from the ABS show that of the 39,000 Australian students who dropped out of school in 2003, 47% of grade 10 dropouts and 36% of grade 11 dropouts were both jobless and course-of-study-less within the first six months!

Financially viable alternatives to dropping out, with better long-term opportunities for employment and development, include:

- switching schools, even if it means paying for public transport;
- studying by correspondence. Distance Education Schools are available in each state, but ensure you only use one that's associated with a TAFE college or university, for example the Open Learning Institute (ph. 1800 657 387), or speak to the careers officer at your local high school;
- asking your school careers officer about workplace training and/or completing senior certificates while working part-time.

ON THE SUBJECT OF MENTORS

It can be very useful to research young achievers from the local business community and for students to complete a brief 'mentorship' or work experience period with them – not only to learn the business side of how they came to be successful so quickly, but also what were the first steps they took out of high school or uni, their misgivings and anything they would have done differently if they'd had the chance. Parents can ask a local businessperson to chat to their child over lunch, or if you're a senior student you could offer to spend a day or two with the businessperson at their place of work.

ON THE SUBJECT OF MAKING 'IT' HAPPEN

Stage one of achieving any financial goal has to include a quick self-assessment of what you've already achieved, including the skills, tools and assets you have at your fingertips, as well as a rough idea of what your options and goals are, before you can sort and prioritise goals into 'goals needed first' and 'goals wanted as soon as possible'. And only then is it possible to form an action plan to help make 'it' happen.

Of course you could also float along aimlessly in life, coping with financial situations as they confront you, or you could do nothing and let financial problems corkscrew you deeper into debt toward bankruptcy and possibly gaol. But to dramatise the repercussions of all three options in a non-financial situation, I like to play with the following scenario:

If you were stranded on a remote tropical island and found three months later by a passing ship, would you expect to be:
a. dead;
b. skinny, naked and covered with infected sandfly bites;
c. lounging on the top floor of your palm-palace with a coconut wine cup in one hand and fresh seafood platter in the other.

Don't laugh, because the question is more relevant than it appears. When I speak to class groups of senior students, the only criticism I ever get about wanting to start your path to success early – and, encouragingly, it's only from a small percentage – is: 'Why would you want to?'

So let me rephrase it: Within three years of completing your final year of study – regardless of whether that's high school, university or trade college – would you expect to be:
a. unemployed;
b. working casual jobs, wearing hand-me-downs and commuting on foot or skateboard;
c. well on the way to debt freedom and early retirement.

If you don't make it happen, who will? (That's Rule 46, by the way.) Some teenage cynics may reply 'Who cares?'. But if you don't care about yourself, how can you expect anyone else to?

> **Rule 44 of my 50 Fun Rules for Success:**
> **Failing to plan = planning to fail.**

STUDENT SELF-ASSESSMENT CHALLENGE

1. Where you're at now

a. Write down everything you own (or that your parents will allow you to take when you leave home) and beside each, write an approximate re-sale value. Include pushbikes, furniture, DVDs, books, CDs, computer games and electrical goods. But don't include clothes or shoes unless you could sell them for more than $10 each. This is your list of tangible assets.

b. Write a list of all your skills and hobbies, with estimates of how much they could help you to earn in the short term. These are your intangible assets.

2. Where you 'need' to be

Assuming a worst-case scenario of having to leave home without parental support, make a list of the things you'd need to survive (as an absolute minimum) for:

a. The first few days, including short-term emergency resources, such as bunking at a friend or relative's place, staying at a caravan park, living out of your car at a camping ground or asking for help from a church or community aid group, plus options for getting around (transport), claiming jobsearch allowance and finding a job. Do not include pay-day moneylenders or pawnshops except as an absolutely last resort, because they usually send you financially backwards much faster than they're worth.

b. The first few months (medium-term), including reliable methods of economical transport and securing your independence. Do you need to buy a car or rent a house first? Your answers will depend on jobs and where they are.

c. The next few years (long-term), including furniture and electrical goods you need, in order of desperation or desire.

3. Where you want to be

Assuming a best-case scenario where everything you plan
works out perfectly, make a list of:

a. Ten things you need to DO to get there.
b. Ten things you need to BUY to make the picture in your head
complete. Maybe your list includes a spa, a tennis court, a
nice car or simply a hammock, a fishing rod and sunscreen.
Never be ashamed of your own definitions of paradise, and
you won't need to waste time, money or effort making
yourself look as if you conform to everyone else's ideals.
c. Ten people or companies you need to help you achieve each
of your major desires.

This is the core idea behind financial goal setting.

4. Action planning

Plan a step-by-step course of action necessary to achieve your
goals. List everything you need to have, get and do. But if you
feel yourself suffering from the negativities associated with
procrastination and over-planning alternative courses of action
to avoid hurdles (for example not starting a business because
you don't know how to fill in a tax return) the cure is to just do
it. Have a go at achieving your goals in order of priority, attacking each step of your action plan in turn. And then attack each
hurdle as you get to it – just like a track star. Don't baulk or worry
about what anyone else is doing. Just concentrate on deciding
what the next step toward where you want to be is, research well
to avoid common pitfalls, and then take it.

9

Standing on Your Own Financial Feet

ASSETS FROM SCRATCH

As independent life after school approaches, you'll be putting yourself ahead of the game if you plan ahead and try to have the following assets accumulated:

- a wardrobe of working clothes suited to your desired job and at least one good set of interview clothes;
- an emergency method of transport, e.g. bike, scooter, taxi or cheap reliable car.
- furniture, including your own bed and perhaps also a cupboard or two, a TV, DVD player, computer and storage chest that could double as a coffee table. By the time I left home aged 21 (having already bought and paid off one block of vacant land) I was able to take with me my debt-free car, a washing machine, ironing board, dining table and six chairs, a set of coffee tables, two large dining room cabinets packed with about $1000 worth of bed linen, towels, cutlery, saucepans and crockery . . . oh, and a garden shed! For several years beforehand, every time some piece of my parent's furniture or white-goods needed replacing, I'd ask if I could buy it and let the family use it until I moved out . . . and I'd been accumulating since I was 10, so my mum ended up missing the furniture more than she missed me. It saved me enormous amounts of time, effort and money in the long run.

INHERITANCES

Children often receive small inheritances in the event of a grandparent or other relative passing away. It's rarely enough to make the purchase of stockmarket shares viable (over

$2000), so what options are there to make the money work as hard as possible? Here are a few suggestions:

- Top up any existing high-interest earning accounts that earn between 4% and 6%.
- Invest in your parent's credit card. If parents have a credit card that is charging them 12% to 19% every month while they're struggling to pay it off, kids can consider loaning the money to them and sharing the savings with them 50:50, earning themselves 6% to 9.5% and helping others in the family too.

Then when the total cash invested into a savings account reaches $2000, see Chapter 13 to read about buying shares in a strong, reliable Aussie company (not necessarily a blue-chip). If shares do happen to interest you, then see your stockbroker.

ON THE SUBJECT OF MOBILE PHONES

It can be very easy to talk yourself into debt these days. That's right, with your mobile phone. Recently a poll conducted by Telstra found that of the 16- to 21-year olds they asked, 31% had rung up more debt than they expected. The key to avoiding this is to choose a plan that's right for you and your usage, and then budget for it. There are so many different kinds of plans now so contact your phone service provider at least twice a year to make sure the phone contract you're subscribing to is the best one for you – and what the costs are if you leave. Here are some other ideas to help you save money:

- **Be a little old fashioned** – if it suits your lifestyle without any loss of personal safely – by not having a mobile phone at all. Use a friend's mobile when you're out with friends, giving them a dollar each time you make a call, and keep a phone-card and coins in your pocket or wallet to ensure you can always use a public phone.
- **Check for company specials** where phone providers give you a discount for calling your friends on weekends, late at night, and/or between phone numbers on the same

network. Ask which network most of your friends are using so you can call them more cheaply than you do now.

- **Call your phone provider** for help in matching your caller habits with a plan, for example, what time of day you make most of your calls.
- **Compare call rates** as well as flagfall rates to see if you'd be better suited to a scheme that charges by the second or one that charges in blocks of 30 seconds. And yes, it's definitely worth being realistic when estimating your usage, because one of the biggest mistakes made by young phone users is in assuming they'll use phones sparingly, then choosing the wrong mobile phone scheme and blowing their budgets time and again.

ON THE SUBJECT OF LENDING MONEY OR BELONGINGS TO FRIENDS

Not a good recipe for achieving your financial goals if belongings keep coming back to you damaged or cash isn't repaid inside the same fortnight it's lent to a friend. Of course you want to be generous with friends and family as often as possible, but making a habit of doing it regularly with items of value can be damaging to your cash flow, as well as frustrating, stressful and irritating if – or I should say *when* – things eventually go wrong. There are few things in life as tragic as a friendship destroyed because of squabbles over money. So learn to say 'No!' in a friendly way, long before it gets to be a worry.

STARTING TO STAND ON YOUR OWN FEET

By the time you leave school, your teachers should have already supplied you with the application forms you need to apply for Jobsearch allowance on the last day of your exams. But if they haven't you can get them from your local community hub (a one-stop-shop for government services, which usually includes officers or agents for Centrelink, the Family Assistance Office, and local council, usually located close to a public library). Or you can get them from Centrelink directly or online from www.centrelink.gov.au. The sooner you get them in, the sooner your payments can start!

EASY-PEAZY 3-STEP BUDGET FOR BEGINNERS

Whether you decide to work full-time straight out of school or go on to tertiary study, whether you are going to live at home for a while or strike out on your own after graduating, you will need a budget.

Step 1: Add up your expected expenses for the year, divide by the number of pays you get in 12 months or the amount of study or other government allowances you're entitled to and that's how much money you have to put into a savings account just to keep your head above debt. It's as simple as that. For example, if you're earning a part-time income while at high school and paying a small amount of board to help out with food, and only have bus tickets and a couple of annual memberships to pay for each year, your total bill expenses might only be $4000. Divide by 52 weeks in a year, means you have to put $77 a week into a savings account. (*Note:* After leaving school and getting your first job, expenses are likely to be a lot heavier on your wallet as responsibilities for clothes, phone calls, power, rates and water swiftly shift from being your parents' responsibility to yours.)

Step 2: Save an extra two whole pays – that's usually enough for a safety net for emergencies.

Step 3: Work out how much you have left over each pay and then share it between:

- a 'sanity' allowance to spend on anything you need to ensure that payday always brings at least a small reward;
- paying off existing debts;
- goal savings to help save for anything that costs more than one pay packet can afford.

And there you have it: your first balanced budget!

Now comes the hard part: attempting to stay on top of it, controlling expenses and practising patience so you don't rush out and buy anything you want, just because all your friends seem to have it.

CREDIT RATING

As a new school-leaver one of the first things you should set your efforts to achieving (after securing your first reliable job or enrolling in further study) is a sound credit record in order to make the purchase of your first home or vehicle possible, since a credit check is the first step in approving your application. This, too, is very easy to do:

1. Never be late in making a bill payment.
2. Apply for a credit card with an interest-free period and use it to buy things that you ALREADY have the cash for, making sure that you pay the card off on the same day or week as the purchase instead of waiting the full month. Ask your parents to buy the groceries with you on your credit card and then have them pay you the cash to pay off the same week or day, to achieve the same result.
3. If the family goes on holiday at a unit booked through a real estate agent, pay for as much as possible in the teenager's name to help build a credit rating through the agent's rental networks as well.

AVOIDING MISTAKES THAT CAN SET YOU BACK A DECADE

- As soon as you turn 18, enrol at your local post office to vote in federal, state and local elections, or face possible fines the next time the rolls are checked.
- If enrolling in tertiary education, try to make some or all of your HECS payments up-front each semester in order to get a 20% discount and lower the chance of starting life after university with debts hanging over your head. Consider getting part-time work to pay for HECS or interest-free loans from parents or other close relatives.
- Don't waste money buying or maintaining a car if you can get by with a pushbike, rollerskates, borrowing a parent's vehicle and/or using public transport.

- Avoid all traffic fines. Every 'dead dollar' you spent on fines equals between $1.20 to $1.80 EXTRA that you have to earn in order to pay for it (because of tax).
- While still on your L-plates, never drive without the company of an open licensed driver, or it will blow your insurance if there is an accident and you risk fines if you are caught by the police.
- If buying a car while using the vehicle as security (to get cheap interest), beware that any repeated driving offences or accidents may prevent you from getting comprehensive insurance, and without comprehensive insurance, you risk losing your car even if you're able to keep up repayments.

A TRICK: SELLING SOMETHING AND STILL HAVING IT
No, I'm not talking about stealing it back again! I'm talking about creating something as a hobby or professional income that you only have to sell once, can have a copy to keep for your own records and can keep selling in order to earn ongoing royalties (practically indefinitely). For example, selling copies of books, illustrations or paintings that you've created, as well as patenting inventions or writing songs and/or music also count as ways to earn ongoing income from one piece of work which you can sell and technically still claim ownership to. Pretty amazing way of looking at things, hey?

Did you know?

In 2003, an 18-year-old student by the name of Helen Oyeyemi, in her first-year at Corpus Christi College at Cambridge, in England, received a £400,000 advance for a two-book publishing deal that included her first novel called *The Icarus Girl*. That puts her in the top-earning bracket of British authors, alongside J.K. Rowling, and makes the record-books as one of the biggest deals for a young author in publishing history! And she's still studying!

ON THE SUBJECT OF HONESTY, FINANCE AND BUSINESS

It's sad to say that in many professional arenas, the term 'business ethics' is treated as an oxymoron – in the same basket as other contradictory conjunctions, such as 'honest politician', 'government organisation' and 'tax assistance'.

However, I deal with hundreds upon hundreds of large and small companies every year, where the staff and managers are not only honest and their businesses thriving, they're also a sheer pleasure to deal with.

Sure, it can be tough watching scum-sucking pond crawlers use deceptive tactics to steal your customers. Of course it hurts to see lying skunks promoted ahead of you, but those people can fill their lives with all the money on the planet – they'll still be empty.

At times it takes guts and determination and more than a handful of tear-stained hankies to stick to your morals and beliefs, but it CAN be done. And even when it doesn't seem to matter to anybody else, it still matters to you.

You wouldn't steal a car just because everyone else seems to be getting away with it. And by the same reasoning you don't have to be dishonest to be financially successful. If you always behave reputably, politely and try to do the best job that you can for your clients, then it becomes more and more difficult for someone to slur your reputation.

A FINANCE QUIZ

By the time you leave school there are lots of things about finance that you're expected to know. And even if you have been taught them, you may remember them or you may not. So the following quiz is a fast and easy way for everyone, from eight-year-olds to adults, to refresh their memories. Parents can do the quiz with kids, or either kids or parents can do it on their own. Each answer goes into a little detail, for younger students, and then more detail for older readers. Upper-primary school aged children may like to make a game of this quiz with their friends or parents. You can either test them over the dinner table or at bedtime, or ask them to quiz you and explain the answers to you when you get them wrong. Secondary students, on the other hand, often prefer to work through the questions themselves and ask questions whenever they need to.

1. Who owns the bed you sleep in every night?
a. My parents – they paid for it so it's theirs.
b. The bank – my parents are paying off a credit card or loan for it so they will only own it after it's paid off.
c. I do. I paid for it myself or someone gave it to me as a present, so when I leave home I can take it with me.

Handy hint: Kids don't need money in order to achieve owner-ship of their bed. Kids as young as five can 'earn' their beds from their parents by making it through a long list of good deeds or chores (on top of the ones they already have to do), which can be spread out over a long period of time. It's a valuable lesson in goal setting, reward for effort and ownership of an asset with a good resale value that they'll continue getting value out of until they have children of their own.

Did you know?
In this book, as in all my books, wherever you see the word 'bank', I'm also talking about building societies and credit unions, except for the rare times when they have minor differences and I explain them separately.

---

2. What's the difference between a bank, a building society and a credit union?
The short answer: Not much any more. Banks, building soci-eties and credit unions can all provide you with most useful kinds of accounts and loans, like savings accounts, term deposits, EFTPOS cards, overdrafts, mortgages, car loans,

personal loans and credit cards. They also exchange currencies for various countries when travelling or trading overseas.

The longer answer for advanced students:

Banks were the first kind of company allowed by legislation to offer wide-scale financial services in Australia. Because they were the first, they possessed the biggest chunk of the market at the time of 'deregulation' in the 1980s (when the banking regulations were cut down to allow fairer competition).

Building societies are financial organisations that originally gained permission from the federal government to compete against the banks for the specific purposes of helping people to buy, build and improve homes using cheaper and more flexible loan products. Deregulation of the banking industry has made it a little easier for them to offer competition to the banks.

Credit unions are cooperative associations that provide cheap loans and high-interest savings accounts, but you have to be a member (or a close relative of a member) of a particular industry to use them (e.g. a teacher to use the Teachers' Credit Union).

3. When talking about money, what is 'interest'?
There are two kinds of bank interest:

a. The money paid to you by a bank as a reward for keeping money in an account with them. The bank does this using 'simple' interest because they want to use your money to loan to other people at a higher rate of interest so they can make a profit. (That means that when you check your balance, the money only looks as if it's sitting in there waiting, because the number you see is the amount the bank owes you if you want to get all your money back from them at once.)

b. The money the bank asks YOU to pay THEM when you take out a loan. This kind of interest gets billed to your account every month (compound interest), making your debt bigger, unless you make your repayments on time. And if you don't pay off your loan very quickly (like in one to five years), then even if you do make your repayments on time, the big or expensive thing you bought can end up costing you twice what it was supposed to.

4. What's the difference between simple interest and compound interest?

Interest is a percentage of extra money payable or owing on an amount of borrowed or invested money (the principal). Simple interest is the amount you'd have to pay if you only received or paid the interest on the principal. Compound interest is paid not only on the principal, but also on the interest after it is due and the amount has been added to the principal.

For example, 10% simple interest per year on $300 is $300 × 10 = $30.

But 10% interest per year on $300 compounded monthly is $300 × 0.10 (interest rate as a decimal) ÷ 12 (months) months in a year = $2.50. You'd add the $2.50 onto your starting balance, so that the next month, the interest is calculated on $302.50 instead of $300, and so on every month until the end of the year when you realise that the total interest that adds up over the year comes to $31 instead of $30.

Handy hint: The magic of compound interest comes when you start talking about really big amounts of money OR very small amounts of money compounded over many years. For example, Chapter 2 shows how you can turn $20 every fortnight into $4.8 million over 60 years even though it's only cost you $31,000. . . the other $4.5 million comes from compounded bank interest!

5. What's a normal bank account?

A place to put your money so you can take it out whenever you need it. They often don't pay much interest because interest is usually calculated on the smallest amount of money you had in the account in the month. For example, if you opened a normal bank account with $1 and put $1000 into it every day, at the end of one month you would have $30,001 saved up, but the bank would only pay interest to you as if you had $1 in the account for the whole month. This is called calculating interest using the minimum monthly balance.

Normal bank accounts often charge monthly fees plus extra fees each time you use the account to put money in or take money out so they are NOT good places to keep ANY money, especially money for your savings.

6. What's a savings account?

A bank account that is supposed to pay you higher interest than if you'd put the money into a normal bank account. It's supposed to calculate your interest based on how much you have in the account every day, even if it only pays you the interest once a month (or once every three or six months). This is called calculating your interest on a daily balance. Savings accounts usually have cheaper monthly fees and let you put money in and take money out a few times each month before they start charging a fee. Some savings accounts even give you bonus interest if you don't take any money out at all.

7. What's an online savings account?

Not to be confused with ordinary savings accounts which can also be accessed using online banking services, an 'online' savings account' or 'online-only' savings account is a new breed of savings account that offers higher than usual interest rates with interest generally calculated on the daily balance and paid monthly. Monthly fees are usually non-existent too. But the trade-off comes by being cheap for the bank to operate because it can only be accessed by phone or the Internet, instead of by passbook over the counter. Some banks also offer access through EFTPOS, ATM or Giropost, while others require that funds must be deposited or withdrawn using a 'normal' savings account and transferred in or out of the online account only by phone or Internet. OSAs are not yet available at all banks, building societies or credit unions.

> *Handy hint:* Normal savings accounts are best suited to day-to-day banking, while online savings accounts are excellent for long-term savings or goal savings – making it harder to get at your money helps you avoid spending it by accident.

8. What is a term deposit?
A special bank account where you can 'lock' your money away for a set period in order to earn higher interest than you would by leaving it accessible in an ordinary savings account. Usually, the longer you lock your money away, the higher the interest rate you earn. You can still get your money back urgently if you need it, but there's usually a fee.

9. What is a cheque account?
Any kind of normal bank account, savings account, overdraft or business account that has a chequebook linked to it, to allow the account owner to write a cheque in order to pay money to someone instead of paying by cash, EFTPOS or credit card. Now that credit card statements are acceptable as tax records, cheque accounts are quickly becoming a thing of the past, thank goodness!

If you receive a cheque as payment you can deposit it into any kind of account, but it usually takes at least three working days to 'clear' (for the money to become available to you). Interstate cheques take up to seven working days to clear and international cheques take 14 to 28 days to clear. If the person who wrote the cheque doesn't have enough money in their account to 'clear' the cheque, it 'bounces'. You get charged a fee and you have to ask for your money again. Cheque accounts are also much more expensive to draw money out of, because the government charges (usually 60 cents) per cheque withdrawal as BAD tax.

10. What is BAD tax?

Bank Accounts Debit tax. Bad by name and bad by nature, it's a tax on withdrawing cash from your bank account whenever you use a cheque instead of cash, EFTPOS or credit card. Governed by each state or territory, the Federal government has repeatedly recommended it be repealed in each state, however at the date of printing, all states still charge BAD tax.

11. What is capital gains tax?

Capital gains tax is a tax on the increase in value of an investment (not counting the official rate of inflation over the same period). You only have to pay CGT when the investment is sold or otherwise disposed of and it can be minimised by deducting the costs of improvements.

12. What is GST?

Goods and services tax is a 10% tax that's added to most commercially sold goods and services and paid to the Tax Office on a BAS (Business Activity Statement) every month or three months, or yearly, depending on how big the business is. Consumers pay GST on most goods and servives, including clothing and prepared foods.

13. What is EFTPOS?

Electronic Funds Transfer at Point of Sale, which means giving a shop's bank accounting system access to your bank account over the phone line so the cost of your purchase can be deducted immediately from your account and deposited to their account within seconds (or overnight after verification).

14. What is a mortgage?

A loan that provides enough money to buy a house, unit or empty block of land before you have enough money saved up to pay for it by yourself. To get a mortgage you have to prove to the lender that:

- you're a responsible person and have enough 'deposit' (cash saved up) to pay off a big chunk to begin with;
- you earn enough money to pay back the loan in 30 years or less (and these days property costs so much that it usually takes two people with jobs to pay them off).
- you'll make repayments every month without missing any, and you have paid off something before, like a car or motorbike. Renting a property, paying electricity and NEVER being late paying any of your bills can help prove you're responsible with money, as can avoiding traffic fines.

One of the nastiest things about a mortgage is that the bank can change the amount of interest and/or fees they charge almost whenever they want (within the limits dictated by the Reserve Bank of Australia) and there's hardly anything you can do about it – especially where the terms, conditions and bank fees are concerned – because even if you change to another bank, they can change either their terms, conditions, bank fees or interest rates whenever it suits them too.

The most amazing tip about a mortgage is that the bank tells you how much you need to pay them every month in order to pay off your loan, but if you pay off your loan faster, you can save hundreds or even many thousands of dollars!

Handy hint: People who have more than one type of debt – for example a credit card, a mortgage, car loan and maybe a personal loan – can sometimes save a lot of money if they consolidate their debts (increase the loan with the lowest interest rate enough so you can pay out the other debts at higher interest rates). But those people will only be better off if they keep paying the same total amount in repayments (at the lower interest rate) or else they can end up paying off the smaller, more expensive loans (as part of their cheaper big loan) for the rest of their life – and end up costing them much more in the long run. To help you work out if 'consolidation' will work well for your particular loans, the Australian Securities and Investment Commission has made a free and very easy to use calculator available for download from their website at www.asic.gov.au.

15. What is a credit card?

Technically, it's the piece of plastic – about the same size as your student ID card. It's brightly coloured so you can't lose it easily in your wallet and it has a coded magnetic strip on the back so reader machines at shops can automatically get paid for things that you're buying. But the words 'credit card' are also used to mean the loan account attached to the card, which has a negative balance and is waiting for you to pay it back. You only have to ask the bank for a credit card account once, at the beginning, when you decide how much you want your maximum loan amount to be. Most people usually start with a limit of $500, $1000 or $2000, but just because you have the loan available doesn't mean you have to spend it – UNLESS you're extremely good at money management AND can pay it off in full every month AND use the points gained by usage in order to earn freebies under an award scheme. Otherwise, it's safest if only used for emergencies.

If you don't buy anything using your credit card, then you don't have to worry about paying any interest or repayments. Credit cards charge really greedy rates of interest that can cost you a lot of money if you use them to buy things but don't pay them off before interest becomes payable. Many cards have 'interest-free periods', so that instead of paying them off by the end of the day, you have until the end of 44 days (or 55 days, depending on the bank) before interest is charged on the amount still owing. A great thing about credit cards is the insurance that usually comes with them to protect you against people who don't send goods that you've paid for over the phone or items that arrive damaged. Other pluses for credit cards include their monthly statements, which provide a clear record of spending, as well as the security and convenience of not having to carry as much cash around.

The biggest misunderstanding with credit cards is that the

minimum monthly repayment is the only amount you have to pay. You must aim to repay all, or as much, of your debt as you can every month or else your purchases will end up costing many times their initial price.

> Just because you have a loan available with a credit card or overdraft does NOT mean you have to spend it like an overpaid moviestar!

Warning: Never let your credit card out of your sight at a shop or restaurant, because it only takes a disreputable shop-person seconds to swipe your card through a pocket-sized computer that reads the magnetic information so that a duplicate credit card can be made later. (The crime is called skimming or cloning and is reported to occur somewhere in the world every eight seconds!)

16. What is an overdraft?

An overdraft is a special kind of bank account that's like joining together a semi-cheap credit card and a savings account that pays high interest, so you can either save money into it, or take money out without using different accounts. An overdraft is just like a loan when it comes to repayments because you always have to keep your repayments going even after you've paid back your loan – but the good thing is that the money for those extra repayments is still yours. They're just like forced savings that you promise to bank every pay (excellent to help you save up for bills, investments or holidays), but with the extra flexibility of letting you take out the cash again as soon as you wish, just like an ordinary savings account!

Few people realise just how useful an overdraft can be. You need to decide the maximum borrowing limit you'd like to have available as a loan for emergencies – like choosing your credit card limit. Usually that's between $2000 and $10,000 for young adults. And if it's approved – based on your income and evidence of how good you already are at saving for assets and paying your bills – the bank tells you how much you have to start paying them every month as a minimum repayment (assuming that you will use the whole amount of your loan straight away and pay it back steadily with interest over the next 2 to 10 years), with the length determined by the agreement you come to with your bank, building society or credit union.

One of the niftiest things about overdrafts is that you don't have to use the loan if you don't want to – and if you don't then you never have to pay any interest. Instead, the bank will pay YOU fairly good rates of interest, just like a term deposit for saving your 'repayments' up as savings instead.

Here's an example: If your car breaks down and you need to pay a really big repair bill, then you can pay for it using your overdraft, which will use up your savings first and then start a small loan automatically for the difference (up to your maximum limit) – and it usually charges less interest than a credit card!

> An overdraft is like a cheap credit card that pays YOU interest every time you get ahead in repayments!

17. What does ATM stand for?
Automatic Teller Machine . . . now do you feel silly calling it an ATM machine? It's the 'hole in the wall' that's linked to bank accounts electronically, so it knows the maximum amount of money each person is allowed to withdraw.

18. What is an employee?
Someone who is paid to do somebody else's work, or who performs work as a team member and receives either a pay packet full of cash, a cheque or a deposit into their bank account at the end of each week, fortnight or month as payment. At the end of each financial year they receive a Payment Summary which totals up all their pay and tax

payments so they can submit a tax return to the Tax Office to make sure they've paid the right amount of tax on their income.

19. What is a financial year?

In Australia a financial year (also known as the fiscal year) consists of all the months from July to June – that's the second half of one calendar year plus the first half of the next calendar year. So all transactions from 1 July 2006 to 30 June 2007 would be referred to as the '2006/07 F/Y'. New Zealand and East Timor use the same fiscal year as Australia, as do Egypt and Pakistan, but other countries use different dates.

Countries	Dates of financial (fiscal) years
Japan, Canada, India	1 April to 31 March the following year
United Kingdom	6 April to 5 April the following year
Iran	21 March to 20 March the following year
USA	1 October to 30 September the following year
France, Germany	The same as a calendar year: 1 January to 31 December

Handy hint: Watch Australian stockmarket prices as the close of each financial year approaches around the world to see how other markets impact on Australian share prices each time major international investors shift their money from investment to investment in the lead-up to help minimise their annual taxes. Sometimes the changes are negligible while some of the broader trends are fairly regular from year to year.

20. What are stockmarket shares?

To oversimplify, stockmarket shares are very small pieces of a big company (or set of companies) that you can buy through an agent called a stockbroker. Each piece can grow in value (or shrink in value) to reflect the growth (or reduction) in value of the company or the country's economy. Many companies also pay interest to shareholders once or twice a year in the form of dividends. Dividends can be franked (which means they've already had tax paid on them by the time the shareholder gets paid, at the rate of 30% which is the current company tax rate), partially franked (only a portion of the tax has been paid) or unfranked (the shareholder is responsible for paying all the tax due on the dividend, just as they would be for interest on a savings account).

21. How much will the government take out of my pay packet when I leave school?

a. Nothing, if your only income is coming from Centrelink.
b. Nothing, if you're an Australian citizen AND you earn less than $6000 for the year.
c. 48% if you don't apply for and get a tax file number from the Australian Tax Office.
d. All other situations depend on how much you're earning in total for the year.

22. How do you tell what is good value for money?

It's partly maths and partly opinion, so there's no exactly correct answer for this unless you're comparing two things that are exactly the same price, quality, durability and have the same warranty. But as a general rule, for anything that costs more than $50, keep your eyes open for at least three quotes (advertised prices) to see if prices and features of the item vary from shop to shop.

Buying something that doesn't depreciate, rot or evaporate can also represent good value for money, because while you may have spent your cash, if you think about it, you also still have it. To get it back, all you have to do is sell the item and you're 'releasing' the equity again. So if you have a choice between buying a treat or lifestyle improvement that's going to lose value or one that's going to either stay the same or increase in value, does this make it any easier to know which is better value for money?

Handy hint: Just because something has a markdown sticker does NOT necessarily make it good value. Very often prices were inflated to start with and have been dropped just enough to attract your attention to the bright yellow sales sticker.

Definition Alert!
Warranty = A promise by a manufacturer or a seller that they'll fix their product if it breaks within a certain period. Warranty periods are often an estimate of approximately how long the manufacturer expects that you can own the product without a breakdown. If the company is a reputable brand, then they'll usually honour a warranty even if the breakdown occurs within a week of warranty expiry anyway! So there's another good reason to base a little bit of your decision on which 'brand' you like, even if it's a few dollars dearer.

---

23. What is a will?
A will, also known as a 'Last Will and Testament', is the signed and witnessed document that you organise as soon as you leave school and start earning an income or accruing assets so that your friends and relatives know exactly what you want to leave to them in the event of your death. Most people don't worry about organising a will until after they purchase their first property or have children. But even minors who have left school early can make out a will.

Wills can be made by speaking to a solicitor (fee negotiable), contacting your nearest office of the Public Trustee (typical fee of 6% of the estate) or buying a do-it-yourself will kit (for under $60) from your local post office or newsagent.

Dying without a will is called dying intestate, which means your nearest surviving relatives automatically get equal shares of your belongings and assets, the sale and distribution of which is organised by a government organisation called the Public Trustee after deducting their fee. And if no next-of-kin exists, then all your money and assets can be forfeited to the Crown (kept by the government).

24. What is a sanity allowance?

A modest percentage of your income or pocket money which is used regularly to spoil yourself with the kinds of personal treats that make living worthwhile and which – by careful budgeting – help you to feel much less stress in having to cut back on other expenditures in order to afford everything you need. For children under 12, the sanity allowance is usually 30% to 80% of their pocket money, with the percentage progressively dropping until adulthood, when sanity allowances are usually 3% to 5% of the weekly income.

Warning: Most people who budget very strictly on low incomes suffer the 'budget blues' if they don't allow themselves a small sanity allowance to help keep the smallest, yet most important, rays of sunlight in their lives.

ACING THE TEST

If your child or teenager flew through this quiz without any worries, they're ready to progress to the next batch of topics in Chapter 10, which can be asked as quiz questions or as reverse questions, where your kids read the definitions out to you to see if you can guess the topic – a great way of getting the information across to them at the same time as recapping things for yourself! And in the meantime, you can use any incorrect answers from this quiz to know where to focus the attention of your new financial literacy program for your children.

10

Advanced Industry-level Literacy for Teenagers

This chapter can be approached in two ways – with topics posed as a quick quiz, or as general reading to help maximise financial literacy in relation to workplace and industry standards and raising awareness of your teenager's rights and obligations within the working adult population.

TOPIC 1: TYPES OF INDUSTRY

- **Primary industry** Just as a primary school is the first level of education, a primary industry is the first level of producing something. Primary industries produce the raw materials or natural resources (e.g. forestry, farming) for making something else (e.g. timber, food).
- **Secondary industry** Just as secondary schools are the next level up from primary, secondary industries manufactures goods from raw materials.
- **Tertiary industry** Any company or government organisation which supplies finished goods, services or infrastructure (e.g. transport companies, private road builders, finance companies and door-to-door salesmen).
- **Private sector** All companies that are not owned or partially owned by the government.
- **Public sector** All government departments and semi-government organisations that are accountable to taxpayers (in part at least) for their decisions and expenditure.

TOPIC 2: TYPES OF WORK

- **Casual work** Irregular work that's done whenever a company needs extra help, or work done by people who

Handy hint: Most industry-related jargon describes itself if you listen to what each word is trying to tell you. Memorising it might help to get you through an exam, but listening to it means you'll understand it.

work hours equivalent to part-time or almost-full-timers. They're amongst the first staff to be laid-off if the company needs to cut back on expenses. A person who does casual work is called 'a casual' and casual staff are paid 'casual hourly rates', which are usually at least 17% higher than permanent rates to account for less stable working conditions and few entitlements. However, changes to work conditions in 2001 made casuals' jobs more secure if they need unpaid bereavement, maternity, paternity or family (carer's) leave. Long-term casuals (employees who've been employed on a regular casual basis for more than a year) have slightly better conditions, being entitled to one year of parental leave on no pay in the same manner as part-timers, as well as five days carer's leave on full pay if a family member is ill, as well as long service leave after 10 years' service (based on average hours worked per year) and rights to dispute an unfair dismissal.

- **e-tailing** Also known as e-commerce, it's selling your services, new goods or second-hand goods over the Internet as a business or professionally run hobby business. This does NOT include spamming, pyramid-selling or any other illegal or disreputable methods of marketing or selling.
- **Freelance** Work that's done by someone who doesn't actually work for a company, but provides the same kind of work regularly for various organisations. For example, journalists can be freelancers if they supply stories to magazines all over the country.
- **Home-based work** Also called 'outwork' or 'homework', this has nothing to do with school. It's unsupervised work that you'd usually do at work, but that can be done

anywhere and, if your employer agrees, you can do it at home instead, making it easier and cheaper to care for young or sick members of your family at the same time as working. Some companies agree to home-based work because it can help to keep the employee productive instead of costing money in sick leave or absenteeism.

- **Internship** A part- or full-time job where you work and receive practical supervised training which is closely related to your career and academic goals. Internships can make it easier to secure full-time professional employment later, since they look good on your résumé! Internships are usually unpaid.

- **Job sharing** When two or more people share a single job and the wage of one person is shared between them in proportion to the hours they work. For instance, if one person works three days out of every ten and the other person works seven, the fortnightly pay packet for a full-timer would be split between them 30:70.

- **Outsourcing** When a company, government department or other type of organisation employs someone outside of their staff to do some of their everyday work. For example, a company that makes tinned food might hire one mechanic to help keep the machinery working as well as look after their fleet of delivery trucks, but if the work gets too much for him, they could outsource some of the truck maintenance to a service station down the street.

- **Overtime** Work performed before or after your usual start and stop times, or on days that you don't usually work (e.g. weekends). This has to be approved by your supervisor so it can be paid at a special higher rate, usually double time or time-and-a-half, but can also be treble time or quadruple time depending on what type of job you have and when the overtime takes place.

- **Piecework** Being paid according to the number of things made or done. For example, someone who stencils T-shirts might be paid $2 for each shirt they finish stencilling.

- **Seasonal work** like onion picking or work at your local show, which is only available at specific times of year.
- **Self-employed** Someone who owns their own company or business and uses their own skills to earn money instead of working for somebody else. The upside is having no boss and greater flexibility to work when it suits you. The downside is you rarely have a regular income and usually end up doing everything yourself and having little spare time.
- **Shiftwork** Working a normal number of hours per day (usually eight), but at a time when most other people are home sleeping or watching TV. For example 5 am to 1 pm and midnight to 8 am would both be considered morning shifts, while 2 pm to 10 pm and 4 pm to midnight would both be considered night shifts. Morning and night shifts normally get paid an extra shift allowance.
- **Technician** Any skilled, non-professional person (no university degree or trade certificate) who has specialist training in a particular method of fixing something, for example a TV technician may be unqualified to wire a house, but accredited to fix the TV.
- **Telecommuting** Also known as e-work. It's commuting to work via the Internet or working at home and having work emailed to you.
- **Tradespeople** Workers who provide physical skills in a specialised industry and usually have to undergo a few years of on-the-job-training as an apprentice, e.g. a mechanic.
- **Traineeship** A learning program within a workplace which employs full-time unskilled staff and pays them at lower 'trainee' rates for a year or two until they are approved as full-status employees. Trainees may also be part-time workers who are still finishing school.
- **Unpaid work experience** Work conducted with school approval during school hours with an employer.
- **Unskilled work** No trade certificate or formal qualifications from uni required. Often basic skills are involved,

e.g. using a cash register, driving, or answering phones. On-the-job training is usually provided.

- **Vocation** A desired profession, job, trade or career.
- **Vocational education and training** Training or education that you get either on the job, on campus, or a combination of both, with the aim of achieving a desired profession, job, trade or long-term career. The term has expanded in recent years to include a wide range of methods of non-campus based training, including workplace training and assessment, completion of secondary level education while commencing full- or part-time work during school hours, vocational graduate certificates and vocational graduate diplomas with possible recognition for any relevant prior learning. For more info, contact your local high school's career officer, or the Australian National Training Authority (ANTA): www.anta.gov.au.
- **Weekend penalties** Special extra payment for time worked on a weekend. For example if you work from 10 pm Sunday night to 6 am Monday morning, you might get paid 2 hours of Sunday penalties (provided it's worth more than what your company pays for working the late shift). It's a rare company that pays both penalties and shift allowances on the same shift.

TOPIC 3: TYPES OF EMPLOYEE

- **Apprentice** A school leaver who earns a percentage of a fully trained tradesperson's wage, earning more each successive year while they continue learning their trade. There is often an element of study at TAFE to many apprenticeships, as well as on-the-job training.
- **Blue-collar worker** Someone who does manual labour to earn a living and whose income is called a wage instead of a salary.
- **Junior** A pay category that's generally based on your age (usually up to age 21), but that can sometimes be based on your experience. Payment is calculated as a percentage of the pay of a full-time, fully-qualified adult employee.

- **White-collar workers** Anyone who doesn't do manual work for a living, e.g. office workers, who traditionally wear white shirts.
- **Work placement** On-the-job work experience which also counts towards gaining a certificate of competency.

TOPIC 4: TERMS RELATING TO PAY

- **Allowances** Small payments made to staff for specific reasons which relate only to that pay packet. Examples include wet pay for having to work in the rain or tool allowance for having to buy and care for your own tools.
- **Annual leave** Also known as holiday pay, this is usually four weeks per year once you've worked a whole year full-time for the same employer.
- **Award rates** A set of minimum wage conditions that are legally binding on employers.
- **Backpay** Money owed to an employee for work they've done and been paid for at one rate of payment, when it should have been paid for at a higher rate. Sometimes back-pays occur when employers are told about increases in basic wages a few weeks after they happen, and sometimes it takes a few weeks for pay officers to work out everyone's backpay.
- **Base rate** Your normal hourly or weekly rate of payment, without including extra allowances, late shifts or penalty rates for working on weekends or public holidays.
- **Basic wage** Often called the minimum wage, it's the minimum amount an employer is allowed to pay you, based on your age, job and experience.
- **Gross pay** The amount of money you earn each pay before tax and other payroll deductions (like health insurance, Christmas club savings and voluntary superannuation) are taken out.
- **Income tax** Also called PAYG (Pay As You Go) tax or pay packet tax, it's the portion of your pay that the federal government demands that your employer takes out of your paypacket. You can get free copies of the tax scales from

your local newsagent. These show how much tax you have to pay depending on how much you earn, how many jobs you have etc.

- **Industrial award** The set of rules that apply to paying all employees who perform a specific type of job. For example, all people who work with electricity, regardless of the company or government department they work for, have to be paid at least the amount of money that's required by the rules for the Electrical Engineering Award (which can be different in each state).
- **Leave loading** A pay bonus (usually 17%) given to some workers while they're on holidays, which works on the theory that staff don't have the opportunity to work overtime if they're away.
- **Payment summary** Also known as a group certificate, this is a piece of paper that provides totals of your income, tax and deductions for the year if you are a PAYG employee. Your employer is required by law to send you a payment summary within 14 working days of the end of each financial year, so you must let your employer know if you change address, even if you no longer work for them. You keep a copy of the PS and send the original to the Tax Office with your tax return for the year.

Did you know?

To find out which state industrial award a job is ruled by, the ACTU has an excellent link on their website for students at http://worksite.actu.asn.au called 'job and union match'. Some of the major rules about pay, allowances, holidays, overtime and other leave for each industry award are also available on this website.

But if you want to check out the nitty-gritty of all the different types of leave and pay entitlements for each industrial award, you can find them on the Internet (www.wagenet.gov.au).

- **Penalty rates** Sounds bad, but it isn't. It's double your hourly rate for work done on a weekend or public holiday. (It can be more, depending on which industry award applies to your job).
- **Perk** An enjoyable, often unexpected, non-monetary bonus. For example, trips to company branches on tropical islands, the use of a company car or something as simple as free tea and coffee provided in your office or shed.
- **Profit sharing** When staff and/or managers get paid a share of the profits as a reward for doing a better than usual job which results in increased income for the company (in the hope they'll do it again).
- **Redundancy payments** A type of golden handshake paid to a worker when they're told that they're no longer needed because their job will no longer exist.
- **Remuneration** Money paid or a benefit given to a person in return for their services. Usually a wage or salary but can also be a special payment such as a bonus.
- **Retainer** Money paid to an outside professional to make sure they are available whenever the company needs them. For example, a lawyer may be a partner in their own company and also be paid a retainer by a football club to help them occasionally with contracts for their players.
- **Salary** Money earned by an employee for continuously working regular hours – usually a white-collar worker. A salary is the amount which an employee is paid per year, but divided equally into monthly, fortnightly or weekly payments.
- **Severance pay** Also known as a golden handshake, it's the money paid by an employer to a staff member who is leaving. The payment usually consists of pay for any holidays or long service leave accrued but not yet taken. It can also include money for needing to terminate the staff member's service at short notice.
- **Superannuation** Also known as 'super', it's money put away, primarily by your employer, to help fund your retire-

ment. It's compulsory in Australia for an employer to place at least 9% of each full-time staff member's gross wage into a superannuation fund, but some employers reserve a higher percentage.

○ **Voluntary super** is paid for by the employee as extra contributions of their own free will on behalf of themselves or their spouse. Voluntary super is the only type of super that can legally be paid back to you as cash before retirement; for example, when you resign or change jobs to a new employer, and only then if it's possible as an arrangement through your employer and super fund. Otherwise super is locked away until retirement.

○ **Co-contributions** are extra superannuation contributions paid into your super account by the federal government for eligible people who earn over $28,000 but under $58,000 each year and who choose to make extra voluntary super contributions which are not eligible as a tax deduction. Government co-contributions are paid at the rate of $1.50 for every extra $1 you pay (up to a limit of $1500 from the government). After 1 July 2007, the thresholds will be indexed to increase each year in line with inflation. For more info contact the Tax Office.

○ **Salary sacrifice** is a portion of your gross (total) pay packet which you might negotiate with your employer to have paid straight into a superannuation account instead of letting tax come out and getting the rest as cash. For example, if you earn $800 a week, tax is calculated on $800, then the tax is deducted and you get the rest in your pay packet to spend or invest. But if you choose to salary sacrifice $100 straight into a super account, then you only pay tax on $700 of your pay packet and the tax on the $100 is calculated at a much lower rate in the super account.

• **Wage** The income earned by a worker (usually a blue-collar worker), based on the type of job they're employed in, what type of work they do and how much work they do from week to week. (See also salary.)

- **Workers' compensation** provides payment of doctors' bills, time off work, therapy and/or medication that might be required following an accident at work – paid for by WorkCover (a special organisation in each state which is operated by the state government but underwritten for insurance by eight approved companies). WorkCover policies are paid for originally by employers in the form of workers' compensation premiums, which are a kind of insurance. And just like insurance, the more claims that are made, the more it costs the employer to pay the premiums. The total number of employees and values of their wages also affect the cost to employers.

TOPIC 5: TYPES OF LEAVE

This topic covers the various valid reasons for not showing up to work but still getting paid (or not getting paid, but not getting sacked or reprimanded). It's especially important for school-leavers or casual employees who are becoming full-time employees for the first time as it provides a broad cross-section of rights and entitlements which are common across most industries – and which are quite a relief to know in advance, because the last thing you need when you're struck by a personal emergency is to worry about losing your job as well.

- **Annual leave** Usually four to six weeks per year, depending on what type of job you have, during which time you receive full pay. Some employers let you split your leave, so you can take it in two smaller batches each year, while other employers let you take it whenever you need to, in batches as small as a day or half-day. (See also Leave loading, page 140).
- **Bereavement leave** A day or two on full pay to attend the funeral of a close relative (including grandparents, parents, siblings and your own children, but not uncles, aunts or cousins), often taken in addition to a few days holiday to help you cope with your loss.
- **Flexitime** A flexible working arrangement that allows staff to start work and finish work every day within a range of

agreed times, instead of at the same time each day. And if an employee works a few long days, the extra hours are 'banked' until they have enough to go home early, arrive late, or stay home for one day. The upside for employees means you can have time off by working it at other times of the week and don't have any pay deducted if you're late because of a flat tyre or late bus. The downside is that you don't get overtime offered very often, if at all. The upside for employers is that staff can get their work done on the busiest days and not be sitting around doing nothing on quiet days.

Did you know?

Some teens and young adults enter the workforce with no understanding that your first meal break can be up to five hours after you start, instead of approximately every two hours, as they are in school.

- **Lieu time** Also known as TOIL (Time Off In Lieu), this is a more flexible version of flexitime, mainly because your few extra minutes or hours of work each day can be 'banked' for longer than a fortnight until you have enough time accrued to take a day or more off.
- **Long service leave** After working for many years with the same employer (usually 10 years but sometimes 15 or 20) you become entitled to LSL, which is usually eight to 10 weeks of extra holidays (on top of your normal annual leave), which can be taken in one big lump to have an extra long holiday or as a few smaller holidays over the coming years, but not usually for periods less than two weeks.
- **Maternity leave** Leave for the purpose of giving birth, with laws providing all Aussie mothers-to-be with rights to a minimum of six and a maximum of 52 weeks leave. Special application can be made with the support of a doctor's certificate confirming excellent health which allows a light-office-working mother-to-be to work up

> **Important note**
> The terms of employment conditions, such as leave, payments and disciplinary actions for breaches vary slightly – or considerably – from industry to industry and workplace to workplace.

until two weeks prior to birth, whereas a more physically active job like a nurse or prison warden will have to stop six weeks prior to birth unless their employer agrees to provide them with safe light duties for the last four weeks. Maternity leave is granted to mothers, while paternity leave is the similar entitlement granted to fathers. Some companies call it all parental leave. In any case, it's basically the right to have (and care for) babies without losing your job, including when adopting. You can also apply to take your paid annual holidays during maternity or paternity leave, but the total time off cannot be more than 52 weeks per birth. (If you have twins, you're not entitled to an extra year for the extra child.)

- **RDO** An acronym for Rostered Day Off. Shift workers can have RDOs at any time of the week or fortnight, sometimes working 10 days straight (or more) before taking the equivalent of at least two days off per week all together as if they were a holiday (without leave loading). Some people who work on remote oil rigs in the ocean, for instance, may work 10 weeks on, four weeks off.
- **Retirement** Permanent leaving of a job, usually because of old age, ill health, or financial independence. Laws against age discrimination restrict the automatic retirement of staff because of their age, provided they're healthy and competent. The old compulsory retirement of men at 65 years and women at 60 years is rarely an issue anyway because tax incentives and structuring of superannuation policies also affect the age people choose to retire, with super policies

allowing employers to make contributions for staff as old as 70. Self-funded retirees – investors who live off their own self-generating incomes – can retire from the workforce as young as they wish, so long as they don't want to access their superannuation policies.

If you wish to retire from the workforce and live off your superannuation policy, then minimum age for lawful fund withdrawal is 55 for both men and women. Even so, the average age of retirement in recent years has been 59 for men and 54 for women. Australians born after 1 July 1960 must also remember that they will be severely restricted in their ability to retire with a lump sum pay-out of their superannuation, in favour of regular 'pension' payments.

- **Retrenchment** Permanent leaving of a job by being officially dismissed because the company can no longer afford to employ the worker.
- **Sick leave** Time off on full pay when you're sick – usually up to 10 days per year, with any extra days taken as sick leave without pay. If you take more than two days off in a row you need to produce a doctor's certificate or the second day's pay could be taken out of your pay packet anyway. If you don't use all 10 days for the year, you can 'bank' them for later years when you may need more than 10. Unused sick days are only transferable if your job moves from one government department to another.
- **Voluntary redundancy** When a company needs to downsize its number of staff it may ask who wants to be first on the list to go, the incentive being a nice fat golden handshake. (Not as fat as what you get paid if you're involuntarily retrenched.)

TOPIC 6: TERMINOLOGY FOR INTERVIEWS, AWARDS AND INDUSTRIAL NEGOTIATIONS

- **Demarcation dispute** An argument between two types of workers over whose job it is to perform a specific task. Demarcation disputes also happen in the home, for example, when two kids fight over the remote control for the TV, based on their age, swiftness and proximity.

- **Employee share plan** A scheme which gives employees shares in the company as a reward for good performance, or allows them to buy shares at a discount. Businesses offer ESPs sometimes because they're a cheap way to reward staff in a way that makes them keen to keep working hard. Employees often choose to buy into an ESP because it's a way to earn extra money, even after they leave the company.

- **Enterprise bargaining** Negotiations between employers and staff to decide on a set of rules and work conditions for their various workplaces within the company, sometimes trading pay rises for better or different working conditions.

- **Induction** A period or process that helps to teach new staff about their jobs within the company. Some companies require only half an hour of induction for new staff, while bigger companies might run induction courses once a week. Induction courses can even run for a whole week or fortnight, teaching new skills to incoming staff.

- **Industrial relations** The relationships between staff, employees and the union representatives who often stand between them as either negotiators or rights activists.

- **Job description** A help-sheet that describes the purpose, goals, tasks and responsibilities for a particular role or employee.

- **Job security** How hard it is to sack you based on the type of work you perform and your terms of employment. For instance a casual employee has less job security than a permanent full-time staff member, especially one who works for a government department, rather than a struggling company.

- **Key Selection Criteria (KSC)** A shortlist of the most important qualities or skills needed by an applicant in order to have any hope at being appointed to the job.

- **Multi-skilling** Training an employee to do the tasks of more than one job. For example an office clerk might shift jobs around the office once a year to gain experience in computer payrolls or stationery control. The upside for staff is that they don't get bored by getting stuck in the same job year after year and also widen their opportunities for promotion. Employers benefit from having 'spare' staff to take over while other staff are on holidays or if someone resigns suddenly.

- **Occupational health and safety** The set of rules, obligations and responsibilities that helps maintain or enhance the psychological and physical health and safety conditions within the workplace for all staff, including employers.
- **Organisational chart** A diagram showing the job structures within a large company or government department, so you can tell at a glance which job supervises which other jobs and how many staff each supervisor is responsible for.
- **Performance appraisal** An assessment done by your supervisor once or twice a year. The review covers everything to do with your job, including the rate at which you take sick leave, your punctuality, efficiency, accuracy, skills and output.
- **Union** An organisation for employees to help them stand up together for workplace conditions, getting better pay and improving security and staff training. Over 2 million Australians are members of the 50 unions which represent different industries. Membership can sometimes be costly, but fees are tax deductible and some unions state their members can earn up to 15% more than non-members do the same industry. And if you're having workplace problems that can't be resolved easily with your employer, a union will represent you in the Australian Industrial Relations Tribunal (AIRC), where objective panels listen to both sides of the story before making a decision.

11

The Sweet 16 – Extra Support Skills to Add Booster Rockets to Your Teenager's Financial Future

It's a fundamental feature of my financial way of thinking that decisions involving money should never be made based entirely on the most profitable or cheapest thing to do. In order to succeed – happily AND with your morals AND sanity AND family intact – you need to include factors that no professional financial advisor can help you with, like balancing the cost or profit of an action against the personal convenience involved, repercussions on those around you, honouring your personal values, coping through emergencies and the fun-factor, to name a few.

So it's extremely valuable for both you AND your children to look beyond the basic skills for handling and making money to find activities that challenge development in other closely related areas as well, for example negotiation, jargon inter-pretation, career planning, rage management and customer service for both sides of the counter.

This chapter discusses the most valuable peripheral skills for helping to maximise financial opportunities at every stage of your child's life after school. I like to think of it as adding booster rockets to your child's shoes while they trudge those first muddy steps in their path to success. So here they are, explained with suggested activities that can be fun and reward-ing for the whole family.

> *Handy hint:* If your child has outgrown traditional bedtime stories but is too young to complete the student challenges, try choosing a student challenge to discuss at bedtime as you're tidying toys away together and tucking them in. It helps to feed their dreams with valuable themes.

1. PRIORITISING WITH/WITHOUT THE FUN-FACTOR

By this I mean being able to have fun AND make financial decisions while considering cost, value, fun and time. This can be applied to all lifestyle related decisions, such as the expense of some sports which also develop team skills, or choosing a lower-paying job because you enjoy it more than a higher-paying job. In fact every lifestyle purchase or decision presents an opportunity for you to discuss one of more of the following points with your financially developing child:

- How much enjoyment or regret (if any) may result from any long-term consequences.
- Toughing out a situation versus taking a quick fix option or researching other choices.
- Taking the consequences of a tough decision head-on versus hoping or waiting for the problem to go away or fix itself.

When finances are tight, your ability to find a healthy financial balance will depend on your skill in prioritising your 'needs' before your 'wants' (with the exception of a small regular 'sanity allowance'), with the additional flexibility of being able to cope even if finances worsen.

> **Student challenge 1: Prioritising**
> 1. Brainstorm the top 10 things that you love to do regularly that cost money. For example horse-riding, playing computer games. Write a list with the most expensive at the top and the cheapest at the bottom, then:

- Draw red circles around your five most favourite or fun things to do.
- Draw black circles around the three you think are the best for your personal development.
- Draw blue circles around the five that are the best value, based on how much they cost, how long they last and anything else that's important to you.
- Now imagine that the money you have available to do these things has just been cut in half for the next three months. As an exercise in prioritising for budgeting purposes, list these items again in order of their new priorities for you. Then write a sentence or two at the bottom to explain which ones you've cut back on, and which (if any) you're able to do more of if you decide to cut back on one or two of the most expensive ones.

2. HONOURING FAMILY, WORK ETHICS AND BELIEFS

It's vital to be able to remain honest and true to your beliefs during business deals, even if a decision helps someone else more than it helps you. This topic is next to impossible to cover in one or two paragraphs, since it encompasses so many things which all hinge on integrity, faith in yourself, faith in others and courage to persevere in the face of adversity. Role models have provided the fastest and most enduring impressions of these for me in my personal circumstances. But the good acts and motivations of sporting legends, young achievers and movie characters can also prove helpful, provided you take the time to discuss them with your child at the time – possibly putting those useless minutes during commercials to good use. (See following page for Student challenge 2.)

3. JARGON INTERPRETATION

It's very useful to be able to read a paragraph of a business letter, technical journal, industrial award or other example of

---

Student challenge 2: Role models

Use a large sheet of project cardboard divided into eight sections. Fill it in with details of eight people who are good role models for each of the following qualities:

1. Handling arguments calmly.
2. Explaining things well.
3. Finishing things on time.
4. Doing things as soon as they need doing.
5. Working hard but knowing how to have fun.
6. Looking after themselves, family and community.
7. Having other inspirational skills.
8. Add another quality that is important to you personally.

If you don't know anyone real or fictional who provides a good role model for you, then use the details for an anti-role-model – someone who is really bad at these things – so bad in fact that they've taught you a good lesson in how NOT to be like them (but change their name!).

Instead of a large sheet of project cardboard, you could make a book of mentors, a bit like an autograph book, but with information about each person and what you find inspirational about them, or use the blank pages at the back of your school diary to do the same thing – with one or two mentors on each page. You can add pictures of your role models and ask for their autographs with personal messages (or write to them) to help inspire you.

---

strictly 'legal language'. You'll understand better by reading each phrase of each sentence and analysing it to find all possible meanings, including the one it means and what it's expecting you to understand without mentioning it specifically.

You will never again have to listen to second-hand reports about rights, entitlements, options or opportunities (unless you choose to) because you can read it for yourself to see if it's true. You can also figure things out for yourself and double check contracts to see if anything sounds suspicious BEFORE you have to send it to legal professionals who charge you by the second. And you can check if your employer is paying you properly and giving you the right amount of holiday pay or sick days by looking up your legal entitlements and reading them thoroughly for yourself.

Student challenge 3: Jargon interpretation

1. Search the Internet for excerpts from the industrial awards for three different types of job, or ask local businesses if you can have photocopies of the ones they use. For example, for an apprentice electrician, look up the Electrical Engineering Award.

2. Read much deeper into the main clauses of each award than you've ever done before – or, if you're using the websites, follow the links to information about each job – to find out the specifics of each job. For example, how many hours per week employees are supposed to work and the times of day during which each shift must be worked; how many days sick leave and holiday staff are entitled to per year, and how much they're supposed to be paid when they work overtime.

3. Now as an exercise in translation, discuss general terminology with your teacher, and then rewrite the clauses for bereavement leave, emergency leave, long service leave, wet pay, tool allowance, maternity leave, paternity leave and study leave WITHOUT any jargon – as if explaining them to a younger friend or sibling.

---

4. GOAL SETTING

Goal setting is especially helpful when teaching children to have three or more goals going at once. For example, a short-term goal for a teen might be saving up for a DVD player, a medium-term goal might be saving up for a pushbike over the course of six months to a year, and a long-term goal might be saving up for their first car. But the challenge doesn't have to be restricted to teenagers; both of my kids began saving for their first cars as soon as they became interested, which was halfway through primary school, and each had more than $1000 saved before their ages reached double digits!

Student challenge 4: Goal setting for the future

Write a list of 10 goals that you'd like to achieve in the first year after leaving high school. Start with personally valuable goals that you may not have achieved yet, like getting a job, starting uni, buying a car or a new surfboard – or perhaps even renting a unit and move into your own place.

Then write down what you need to do to achieve them. Try to think of unusual (but still legal!) ways to reach your goals. Then figure out which ones you're able to do now, without waiting – and race to see if you can achieve them before the end of the year. This can be fun and surprising if you brainstorm it with your teacher and class.

---

5. CAREER PLANNING

Like goal setting, career planning helps to make the path easier if you know where you're heading first so you don't waste time, money or effort doing things you don't need to do.

Student challenge 5: Career planning

1. Make a list of 10 different jobs that you would like to do if you had more than one lifetime to explore them.
2. Make another list of 10 jobs that you would do to earn money if you had no other choice.
3. Write down five hobbies that you have – or would like to learn – that would help you to make a little bit of extra income, for example woodwork, painting or sculpting.

Handy hint: Use the *Yellow Pages* to help you think of jobs that you might not have considered and brainstorm with your class, family or friends.

6. CONTINGENCY PLANNING (CHANGE MANAGEMENT)

Very few things are financially scarier than being in a secure and relatively enjoyable job for a long time, having it ripped out from underneath you through no fault of your own, and having to survive financially while starting again from scratch. Starting a new family or suffering a major injury also count as major changes that can benefit from learning a few skills in 'change management'. Contingency planning – looking ahead, foreseeing possible trouble and setting up general strategies to cope for a wide range of emergencies – therefore ranks among the most important skills to understand, because it includes a number of smaller steps and strategies that can help you, including:

- keeping at least one month's worth of pay packets stashed away as emergency money;
- getting ahead in loan repayments as soon as possible as an extra safety net;
- thinking of food in the cupboard as an emergency resource to save money during a temporary loss of income;
- investing in learning the basic skills of a job that's needed in virtually every town. At the low-skill end of the market, for example, there's bartending, child-minding and service-station-attending, while at the more expensive and more time-consuming end of the job market, there's nursing, teaching and building trades, which all have strong demand for casual and part-time staff, providing invaluable opportunities to you if you're no longer able to work full-time.

Student challenge 6: Change management
- Ask permission to empty your parent's grocery cupboard onto the kitchen bench (cleaning out the crumbs, dead moths and empty packets as you go) and make a list of all the food or ingredients that's available.
- Make a list of meals that you could make to survive for as long as you can without buying any more groceries.

- While cleaning out the cupboard, pretend you find an old cookie jar with $50 in it. Make a list of food you could buy to make your food supply last an extra three to seven days.
- Don't forget to stack everything back in neat rows.

7. RAGE MANAGEMENT

Oh man, isn't this one a toughie! If only rage had a switch you could turn on and off whenever you wished, especially where other people are concerned! But since it doesn't, it helps to learn and practice a few coping strategies for the workplace where your ability to cope with stress, dishonesty and injustice can be directly related to how much income you earn. There are three main tactics that can be helpful when things make you angry:

1. Learning to look at the problem from the other person's point of view and maintaining your sense of humour for as long as possible in a dispute.
2. Venting your frustration or anger through safe physical exertion, such as a workout at the gym, yoga, jogging up and down steep hills, or kickboxing a punching bag in your garage. The time you take away from the problem gives you time to process your feelings and think things through. If you need to do this, make sure your children get to see you working through your aggression responsibly.
3. Setting a good example for your children by handling confrontational events calmly and withdrawing from arguments that look like they could get out of hand. Explain to them the potential damage to business reputation, loss of income, time wasted in arguments and legal fees or court costs to settle disputes through official channels.

Student challenge 7: Rage management
Arrange tables to simulate a shop counter and have fun taking turns at role playing these rage management scenarios.

1. Rational shopkeeper with young children playing on floor behind counter when approached by aggressive, angry customer who bought a product they're not happy with.
2. Rational shopkeeper – tidying toys in his own children's toy area while they're at pre-school – when approached by an aggressive, angry customer who has their own young, frightened, angry or crying children in tow.
3. Grumpy customer with a valid complaint, who approaches an already very grumpy shopkeeper who gets angry at the thought of a refund.

Handy hint: When customers or staff complain about something, there's nearly always something else that's been bothering them – often it's a long string of bad things – and it's common that the problem they've exploded over is just the straw that broke the camel's back. Calm and professional attempts to remedy an unfair situation, asking questions and allowing the other person to vent their steam, will nearly always help to soothe a bad situation quickly. (Always insist on civil language around children.)

8. CUSTOMER SERVICE

Good customer service relies on the following traits, which help to boost financial success in many indirect ways:

- Genuine interest in providing the best service possible so others appreciate your efforts.
- Being diligent and taking pride in your work to achieve personal satisfaction in everything you do.
- Trying to see problems and challenges from another person's point of view.
- Doing something extra to make the experience as enjoyable as possible for both parties, at the same time as building business opportunities and a good reputation.

Student challenge 8: Customer service
Take notes for a week of all the good things you notice shop-keepers or people in customer service positions doing or saying to make your experience a pleasant one. Then try to think of three more things that would improve matters, as well as the reasons why these extra suggestions may be not be in use already, for example expense to management or legal restrictions.

---

9. CASH HANDLING AND CHECKING CHANGE

When money's tight, as it always is with children and teenagers, every coin counts. Practice with cash handling, rounding and coin recognition can go a long way to ensuring every coin works hard. Most parents help with this to a large degree by sending their older kids into convenience stores to buy small purchases and compare prices.

Encouragement and acknowledgement of the child as an independent consumer during the early stages of their retail life does wonders for their confidence in being responsible enough to handle money.

Student challenge 9: Cash handling
See Coin Games on page 199, and *Did you know?* on page 10.

---

10. PRIDE, INITIATIVE AND WILLINGNESS IN YOUR WORK

These are intangible qualities that your child should be learning throughout school by working neatly, quickly, accurately and gaining recognition for their efforts from teachers as well as parents. While these are not 'skills' that can be practised in a traditional sense, they do need to be mentioned here because the differences between fast financial success, struggling year after year and surviving either of these happily is often measured by how much of each of these qualities you allow yourself to express in the workplace or world of business – even in the face of slack work companions, lousy pay or bad management.

Student challenge 10: Pride, initiative and willingness

Write one sentence or paragraph to describe something you've done that:
- you're really proud of, even if nobody else seemed to appreciate it;
- nobody else thought of doing, but you did anyway to solve a challenging problem, stop a problem happening in the first place or because you knew you could do it and didn't mind giving it a go;
- you really hated doing, but you did anyway to get it over and done with.

---

11. NETWORKING

This is the skill of learning how to meet new people who can (or may in future) boost your business, employment or investment status. Networking is one of the fastest and cheapest ways to open doors to new financial opportunities.

It's surprising how often a networking meeting (usually a lunch, conference or seminar at a trade show) can help you meet that one person you've been looking for without realising it – whether it's you who's able to provide a profitable service to them, or vice versa. Parents can help illustrate the importance of this by making sure the whole family knows about any amazing meetings you've had through networking. The following role playing game for their class will also help.

Student challenge 11: Networking

This works best with one, two or three classes of students from different subjects, but can also be done with sporting clubs, scout groups or girl guides.

Preparing for the meeting
- Each student writes down the names of two professions:
  1. The job they want after finishing school.
  2. A job chosen randomly from a hat (after brainstorming jobs from every letter of the alphabet, assigning each job and each student a number to write down onto a slip of paper, tear off and pass forward).
- Make three to 10 business cards for each of the two professions with your name, job and fake phone number on the front (and a logo or catchy slogan if you wish).
- For both professions – the real goal and the role playing job – write a word or two on the back of each business card that describes a major project or string of small projects that your company might be aiming to do.
- For both jobs think of a technical snag that your company is likely to come up against – but don't write it down. Keep it for discussion during 'networking'.

Conducting the networking meeting
- Choose a handful of students at random as 'guest speakers' to explain who they are, their company's projects, and the challenges they're trying to overcome.
- For the rest of the class, each person stands up briefly to announce their name and their two jobs.
- If you hear the names of any jobs that you could use or provide a service to for your own two jobs or companies, then jot down a note of those people's names and make a mental note of what they look like. Then mingle with them, trying to make it to at least 3 and up to 10 people in 10 minutes to see if any of your goals and snags can help each other – and, if so, exchange business cards.
- Discuss your successes, then mingle again for 10 more minutes to meet 10 more new people, again swapping business cards with anyone who would make a good business partner or client. And report again on your success.

12. NEGOTIATING AND BARTERING

Also known as backyard bartering, swap-meets, mates' rates or chalking up a UOME (opposite to IOU), this topic is helpful in demonstrating how nearly everything you have and nearly everything you're physically able to do (especially by way of a skill or hobby) can be used instead of money to help your child advance financially faster than they would otherwise during early stages of their financial career by relying on money alone. Sophisticated bartering for businesses is now also available in Australia and internationally through bartering agents such as Bartercard (www.bartercard.com.au), which make it possible to trade in small to very large values of goods, services and real estate by trading your goods (at cost price) into the 'pool' and choosing the various items you need from other dealers in the network until you reach the same value. For example, a butcher may promise $5000 worth of fresh meat into the network in order to buy a new cold room and cash register, while two or three small pie companies may like to promise $1000 worth of hot pies into the network in order to obtain the meat. And, no, this fresh meat isn't sitting around somewhere going rotten. It's promised as a 'trade dollar' value, so other network businesses can claim fresh meat from the butcher whenever they want it until the total promise to the network has been honoured. But just like any business expenses or purchases, formalised bartering must comply with all tax regulations by keeping detailed invoices, ABN records and processing GST. And for income tax and tax deduction purposes, one trade dollar is equivalent to one Australian dollar.

A warning about GST: Since the introduction of GST, the Tax Office requires that any swapping or major discounting of goods or services during bartering for business purposes has an extra 10% portion set aside and sent to them as payment for GST. For example, if I swap a car worth $80,000 for computer equipment worth the same amount including GST, then no money would change hands between me and the other guy. But I'd have to send $8000 cash to pay the Tax Office AND I'd have to claim back $8000 from the Tax Office for the computer.

But if you're a private individual, swapping private goods and hobby talents for other private goods or hobby services (or for minor company services with someone who earns less than $50,000 a year and hasn't registered for GST), then you can conduct your bartering and negotiating of major discounts (in exchange for goods) without having to worry about paying GST. So anyone who is trading their professional skill or products from their business for something from a private person who doesn't have to report on GST will be at a 10% disadvantage during the deal, because they will have to pay GST without getting GST money back for the thing they're swapping for.

Student challenge 12: Negotiating and bartering
Using the roleplay professions from Student challenge 11: Networking, have fun pretending to buy and sell their goods and services (hopefully with an outcome of fair value for both parties, not attempting to rip each other off).

Each student should try to match the skills or products of both their goal profession and their roleplay profession to those of other students with the aim of getting things done around their house that they'd ordinarily have to pay for.

See if you can find 10 other students in your class to barter with and report your experiences at the end.

Handy hint: For younger students, conduct your role playing scenario assuming that GST doesn't exist. Senior students might like to do it three times: once between private parties without GST, once between business partners with GST and once mixing business with private purchases.

13. SURVIVING WORKPLACE PERSONALITIES

No job is heaven every day, just as no school day is. And even if your child's first job does happen to be fun and rewarding most of the time, it's likely they'll have run-ins with some difficult personalities at some stage during their first 12 months. If they can't learn to look at such situations light-heartedly or tough it out long enough to find another job, it can be dangerous for their financial future. As a parent, you need to remind your new income earners that:

- the first six months of any new job are always the toughest;
- your door is always open if they need to talk about workplace disputes;
- it takes a full year to figure out which (if any) of the other staff have disruptive personalities.

Student challenge 13: Workplace personalities

Developing your sense of humour to cope through difficult people problems often makes the difference between persevering long enough to achieve significant financial benefit or chucking in a job to start from scratch somewhere else.

- Try thinking of the most aggravating person you've ever known. Give them a fictional name.
- Imagine that you're both cartoon characters and a cartoonist is writing a funny fight scene for children about you.
- Make a list of five funny things that would happen in the scene. Draw it into a comic strip using stick figures if you wish or write a fun short story to help vent your frustration. Stick it into your private diary where you'll always be able to look at it and know that such antagonistic people are laughable.

---

14. ASSERTING YOUR RIGHTS AS A CONSUMER

'Dear sir, your company sucks . . .'

Not a good way to get what you want. Not a good way to

Handy hint: To double-check that you're in the right in a consumer dispute, try explaining the situation to a friend or workmate to see if they think you're being reasonable. If you're still not sure, contact the Australian Competition and Consumer Commission (ph. 1300 302 502 or www. accc.gov.au), which can also provide information to help negotiate the honouring of warranties and refund policies.

teach your children to assert their consumer rights either, whether it's by phone complaint or in a letter. You can train your children in the basics of fair and equitable dispute resolution by encouraging them to calm down after a family dispute and explain to you in short sentences:

- who the dispute is against;
- what the dispute is about;
- their preferred solution as well as one or two other possible solutions that would make them semi-happy in case they have to compromise.

Ensure that all parties involved are allowed to voice their responses to the same question without interruption – including you, who as both the parent and the adjudicator also needs time at the end to voice your frustration at why the dispute is causing family distress.

Many times in business disputes – as in family disputes – it's a simple matter of one party not being aware of the needs or problems being experienced by the other. Other times, unemotional diplomacy will be needed to achieve resolution through official channels, especially if your initial explanation does not result in an offer to fix the problem.

Student challenge 14: Asserting your rights as a consumer

Role play 1: You recently purchased a laptop computer that doesn't work properly. Roleplay a phone conversation with your family, friends or classmates to explain the problem and ask for a replacement. The sales assistant role plays that they need a little convincing, but they eventually agree.

Role play 2: The sales assistant is incompetent or unhelpful. Role play a second phone conversation attempting to speak to their manager, who is unavailable.

Role play 3: Write a one-page letter to the manager stating what the problem is, quoting dates and conversations and asking the manager to look into the matter and get back to you promptly by phone or email.

Role play 4: Write a follow-up letter asking why the manager has not responded to your letter, or has responded but told you that the laptop you bought is no longer their responsibility. Leave all emotion out of your letter and make no threats. Just state the facts. Research consumer affairs websites as well as looking at the ASIC website (fido.asic. gov.au) to determine:

a. what obligations they have to provide a fair and equitable service to you;

b. what steps you can take when they don't.

Then quote the relevant laws in your letter with a closing statement saying you hope the company will be able to help you rectify the problem at their earliest possible convenience.

15. RESPECT FOR LAWS AND OBLIGATIONS TO THE TAX OFFICE

Most parents know what it's like to earn enough income to throw their tax obligations up into the 30% tax bracket. It doesn't take much. And having to pay roughly one-third of your income to the government can be extremely frustrating! But it's vital to ensure your child understands that temptations to try naughty ways to earn extra income without mentioning it to the Tax Office will get them into trouble when the Tax Office finds out (whether it's this financial year, next year or seven years from now). The fines, penalties and hassle involved will cost you or your child far more than it's worth.

It's much safer to know what's allowed as hobby income. To check, you can look up the Tax Office website at www.ato. gov.au to see the full range of rules for profitable hobbies. Then choose a shortlist of your most desirable hobby opportunities before contacting your family's accountant to double-check the specific rulings for your shortlist. That way you'll get good help from your accountant without wasting much of their time, or missing opportunities that you mightn't otherwise have noticed without checking the ATO website for yourself.

Student challenge 15: Tax scales for your pay packet

Assuming you are an Australian citizen but you don't have any tax deductions for donations to charities or work expenses, the following PAYG tax scales will apply to your situation. Use them to work out how much tax you would pay per year if your total annual income was $5000, $25,000, $55,000 and $65,000:

- If you earn less than $6000 a year, you don't have to pay any tax on your income.
- If you earn between $6001 and $21,600 per year, you don't have to pay any tax on the first $6000 but you DO have to pay 17% on the income between $6000 and $21,600.
- If you earn between $21,601 and $52,000 per year, you don't pay any tax on the first $6000, but you DO have to pay 17% on all income between $6000 and $21,600, (which is $2652) PLUS you have to pay 30% on the rest from $21,601 onwards.
- If you earn between $52,001 and $62,500 per year, you pay nothing on the first $6000 plus $2652 for the 17% tax bracket PLUS $9119 for the 30% bracket PLUS 42% on the rest.

- If you earn over $62,500 you have to pay $2652 for the 17% tax bracket PLUS $9119 for the 30% bracket PLUS $4409 for the 42% bracket and then a whopping 47% tax on the rest.
- If you forget or refuse to apply for a tax file number from the Tax Office you'll have to pay 48% on the whole lot!

You'll also have to pay 48% tax on your investment income IF you're under 18 years of age AND you earn more than $772 per year from investments in your name (instead of working for it), UNLESS one of your parents claims your investment income on their tax returns as income they've earned on your behalf.

16. DRESS REHEARSALS

Great news! Having handled the first 15 of these rocket-boosting skill topics, your mini-moguls-in-training would have advanced their experience with a few extra skills including practice and role playing with:

- telephone skills;
- problem solving techniques;
- professional diplomacy;
- research skills.

And by role playing the student challenges for networking and rage management with full 'costume', like actors conducting a dress rehearsal for a play, they'll also gain practice with:

- presentation skills;
- public speaking;
- hosting skills for a major business seminar/networking event.

Handy hint: Prepare your children for responsible conduct in the workplace by rewarding them in the home each time they see a problem, fix it without being asked and report their efforts to you later.

BONUS SKILL: CREATIVE THINKING

This is an extremely handy skill for helping you spot opportunity where nobody else can by using the skills you've learned so far in this chapter. Creative thinking means finding a new way of looking at a problem or challenge, and a good way of applying this can be to watch what media reports suggest that everyone else is investing in, then looking for other opportunities. To practise using creative thinking and problem-solving skills, try the following mini-puzzle as an exercise in switching on your 'opportunity receptors'.

THE CASE OF THE GARDEN STATUE:
You're in a shop. In your wallet, you have a credit card, a dirty tissue, a membership card for the local cinema, an EFTPOS card, a chequebook and cash totalling $1000. You see a really big statue of a hand giving the V-for-Victory symbol that's nearly as tall as you and costs only $100. You'd love to stick in your front garden to make you feel good every morning as you leave. But you realise that if one of the fingers gets broken in the back of your car on the way home, you'll end up giving your neighbours and everyone who passes by the finger. Aside from getting the store to deliver it safely to your garden, what opportunity is already in your wallet to protect it?

Handy hint: If you've read the mini-puzzle once or twice and still can't come up with at least one possible solution, then be brave and try switching on the other half of your brain to the one you've trained yourself to use. Think about the problem while you're either standing on your head, lying on your side, lying on your back, sitting on your desk, turning your chair to face the back of the room, rubbing your tummy, doodling, pretending to wash (or really washing) yourself in the shower using the 'wrong' hand. Then try again.

Answers are limited only by your imagination, knowledge of your financial resources (or ability to throw more money at the problem), for example:

- You could use the cash to hire a van-taxi or courier to collect and deliver the item for you, relying on the delivery provider's insurance to protect the item for damage/replacement until arrival and placement in your garden.
- You could pay with a credit card, which may have built-in insurance to protect the item until delivery and/or safe arrival.
- You could go home and organise a working party of friends or neighbours to help by using one of their larger vehicles.
- You could use the tissue, bank notes, EFTPOS card, cinema card and rubber bands from around the money bundles to help brace the weakest finger joints as you drive it home in your own car.

What other ideas did you come up with?

12

The GAP Years – Young Adults aged 18 to 21

Once you've left school, your lifestyle and financial choices are even greater – get a job, pursue further studies, see the world or a mix of all three. Living expenses and nesting urges are also attacking with greater urgency too. So this chapter aims to cover as much ground as possible in helping you and your child meet these challenges, but still focusing on the teenagers and young adults who are living at home.

WORKING HOLIDAYS

The best way to see the world is to have someone else pay for it of course – as a defence force reservist, an English translator, a nanny (Aussies are very popular in England!), a missionary or exchange trainee teacher, many of which require only partial education or training. With an employer paying your main travelling and accommodation expenses, you don't lose any income while you're away. Additional jobs such as bartending in the UK, fruit picking in France or working in the ski-fields in the US are also regularly available for Aussies with only basic skills. Special tax rules apply to nearly all foreign income, however. Sometimes you may have to pay tax both in Australia AND the country in which the income was earned, especially if you were working overseas for less than 91 continuous days. In other instances, you may not have to pay any tax on your income at all – as is the case with any Aussie residents who perform work in a developing country for the purposes of helping to develop their infrastructure, since they can be subject to a 'Memorandum of Understanding' (an MOU), which means they don't have to pay ANY income tax either in the country who signed the MOU agreement or Australia. Australia has signed MOU agreements with Thailand, the Philippines, China, Nauru, India, Korea, East Timor and Taiwan, to name a few. (For more info on tax for foreign income contact the Tax Office.)

Working holiday visas for Australian citizens are available in several countries, but usually have age limits (e.g. Canada and Korea 25, Ireland 29 and the UK 27). There are sometimes rules about not working in the same industry as the one which employs you in Australia, but many countries make exceptions for nurses, nannies, therapists, teachers, emergency workers, vets and/or some specialist medical technicians.

Helpful resources with offices in Australia
- Overseas Working Holidays: www.owh.com.au
- Backpacker Essentials: www.backpackeressentials.com.au
- Youth Hostels Australia: www.yha.com.au

Helpful internet resources overseas
- www.workingholidayguru.com
- www.jobmonkey.com
- www.payaway.co.uk
- www.japan.org.au/wvisa.htm
- www.learn4good.com/jobs/
- www.workpermit.com/
- www.livein-jobs.co.uk/free.html

Did you know?
When travelling overseas, a $52 Youth Hostels Association membership and an $18 STA International Student Card can often save you more than triple their cost!

VOLUNTEER HOLIDAYS
These are the next best thing to working holidays, except without the pay packets. If you're lucky you'll get a comfort-

able, safe home with a little regular pocket money – but not enough to live on, buy luxuries, do extra travelling or budget as savings. There are a wide range of opportunities available, though, so here are a few examples – some of which you have to pay for, sometimes costing you more than if you'd organised a tourist trip by yourself.

GAP Activity Projects (GAP) Ltd (ph. 03 9826 6266, website: www.gapaustralia.org) is an educational charity that offers 17- to 20-year-olds the opportunity to live and work overseas for up to a year as volunteers but receiving full board, accommodation and often weekly pocket money with additional opportunities for independent travel. GAP volunteers gain independence and discover the world by living and working in a different country and culture, usually while taking a break from study to grow in confidence and widen perspectives while helping others. But GAP volunteers aren't completely subsidised so you'll need to budget at least $5000 yourself. But it's life experience as well, so you have to balance that against the costs involved.

Many charities, including the Fred Hollows Foundation and the Cancer Council, run trips to raise funds and allow participants to experience new cultures and help others. There are also two semi-government funded initiatives that source international volunteer opportunities: GoVolunteer (ph. 03 9820 4100, website: www.govolunteer.com.au) and Australian Volunteers (ph. 03 9279 1763, website: www.australian volunteers.com).

LIFESTYLE ISSUES – BOOZE, ENTERTAINMENT AND HOBBIES

If your teenager or dependent young adult hasn't done it yet, it's time to encourage them into goal setting and shedding a few of the nasty habits they may have picked up. Take smoking for an example. A typical pack-a-day habit can cost between $250 and $300 per month, which comes to $108,000 over the next 30 years – but if they quit smoking and use that same $300 as extra repayments off a $100,000 mortgage at 8% over the same period – even without the costs of inflation, it's enough to save them a little over $154,800 in interest!

It's easy to spend more money on yourself when you're living in low-cost accommodation with all your living expenses, utilities and meals subsidised by loving (albeit somewhat crazy) parents. So, as parents, it doesn't hurt to help children along the way to forced/compulsory savings – if they aren't already saving by themselves that is – by adding a 'savings portion' to any existing 'maintenance fee' (which is a contribution from their pay packets to help pay for their share of household utilities like power, phone, gas, rates and water or living expenses, like food and toiletries). That way you can guide them in saving and investing a little – with their permission of course – until they feel comfortable, confident or mature enough to take over the portfolio themselves.

Without basic saving skills, your child has no bill saving skills and without bill saving skills, they're destined to a life of pay-to-pay survival strategies, which is only a couple of speeding tickets, a missed phone bill and an overdue rent payment away from being financially destitute.

ON THE SUBJECT OF HOBBIES AND BUSINESS PAPERWORK

Hobby income is not usually taxable, but laws and guidelines are extremely complicated and fuzzy, especially for hobby incomes between $5000 and $20,000 per year. So it's always wise to consult your family accountant to make sure your hobby is okay to stay as a non-taxable hobby as soon as you start earning more than $1000.

- If you wish to claim a tax deduction for costs to run your income-earning hobby, then you have to declare the income as taxable.
- Once your hobby starts earning over $50,000 a year, you have to collect and pay 10% GST.

- If your hobby is very similar to your normal job – for example a car mechanic who also fixes boats on the weekends – then the Tax Office may declare that your hobby is just extra income in the same industry and demand tax, no matter how little extra you earn.
- The amount of time and effort you put into earning the hobby income may also affect whether the Tax Office chooses to tax your 'hobby income' or not. For instance, someone who lovingly restores vintage cars may make $20,000 every second or third year as a hobby, while someone who sells $200 craft every weekend may have to declare it as a taxable business income.

So it also helps to keep basic business records for *any* hobby which begins to earn close to $1000 for the year. That way, you'll have records to help you claim tax deductions for your expenses and minimise the tax, if the Tax Office does decide to rule that your hobby is actually a business. And if you do wish to shift your hobby up a few gears into a part-time or full-time business, then check out the Tax Office's amazing web-portal for new businesses at www.ato.gov.au for all the tools and info you need, including free software.

Basic hobby business records to help work out tax deductible percentages of expenses include:
- a vehicle log book, available from newsagencies, (unless using actual receipts or depreciation methods to claim vehicle expenses, see *Tax Pack* for details);
- a telephone log book, available from newsagencies, filled out in accordance with the *Tax Pack* instructions;
- a list of all utility expenses, such as power, water and rates, then work out a percentage for tax deductibility, for example, if your office is 10% of your floor plan, then 10% of power may be attributable to the business;
- three envelopes for storage of invoices paid by cheque, cash and credit card;
- a folder of bank statements, reconciled by writing and

completing the following formula onto the bottom of each statement;

- a 'cash book' which in its simplest form is a notebook or spreadsheet that details your cash received for the month, (with the total row and total column double checked to make sure they're the same, for example:

Date	Action	Goods Sold	New Capital	Sundries $	Details	Bank Interest	Total Banked
9 Jul	Transfer		$10.00				$10.00
23 Jul	CHQ Deposit		$50.00				$50.00
24 Jul	Cash Deposit	$235.00		$110.00	Refunds of goods returned		$345.00
	TOTALS	**$235.00**	**$60.00**	**$110.00**			**$405.00**

- a 'payments book', which in its simplest form is another notebook or spreadsheet which lists all your expenses in columns such as: office expenses, equipment to depreciate, vehicle expenses, insurances, bank interest and fees charged, tools and sundry expenses. Available pre-printed from newsagents.

How to balance your bank account or credit card at the end of the financial year:

Step 1: Open your cheque book (if you have one) and make sure all cheques appear on your statement. Tick them off.

Step 2: Make sure all deposit receipts appear on your statement, ticking them off as well.

Step 3: Write the following note on the bottom of your last statement for the reconciliation period and fill it in, using details appropriate to your account. For example, the note following is for an overdraft account which is used to buy and sell shares, using a fake account number 123123 S10. With an opening balance of $8115.71 owing to the bank, at the beginning of the year, followed by cash deposits during the year which total $137,865.02, less payments of expenses during the year of $124,939.47, leaving a carryover balance for the next financial year of $4809.84 in credit.

```
OVERDRAFT RECONCILIATION:
O'draft A/C 123123 S10:
Opening Balance @1/7/2006:              -$8,115.71
   plus CASH DEPOSITS (total from
      cash book)                        $137,865.02
   less PAYMENTS (total from
      payments book)                    $124,939.47
O'draft A/C closing balance @ 30/6/2007:  $4,809.84

ALL AMOUNTS CROSS CHECKED
   AND CORRECT:                          $4,809.84
```

Notes:

- The total from your cash book = Total of deposits on your statement.
- The total from your payments book = Total of withdrawals from your statement.
- The most common mistake in balancing your bank account against your cash/payments book is forgetting to add bank interest and fees.

CAR INSURANCE AND BETTING AGAINST YOURSELF

Taking out car insurance is a lot like betting that you're going to have an accident. Yikes! How scary is that? Not nice to think about – and even worse when you see how much your child will be charged by most insurance companies when they tell them they're under 25 years old! What can you do?

You'll have to shop around insurance companies. Every year, they recalculate how much they're going to charge each age group of drivers and each brand and make of vehicle (depending on which categories have made the biggest claims in the previous year). So 17- to 25-year-olds are wise to get used to picking up that phone every year for quotes.

Often, parents will insure a child's car in their own name, but if the insurer asks you to nominate your driving age kids who are regular drivers of the vehicle you're insuring, then don't risk having future claims denied and all your premium payments consequently wasted. Give all the names and ages of the possible drivers in your family (even if it costs a little more), or choose an insurer that doesn't need you to disclose the details of the younger drivers, but does apply a large excess in the event of an accident.

Extra note for teens who like to modify their cars into hotwheels: Many insurers won't cover cars that have been modified because the improvements make the vehicle more susceptible to theft or damage. And if you void the insurance on your car – or if you can't get insurance at all – then you may not be able to get a car loan, which may force you to take out more expensive types of loans or face having the vehicle repossessed!

13

Investment Options, Banking and Packaging

Sick of stumbling around the forest of financial products with your eyes closed? There are so many to choose from, especially when you start looking for places to stash away cash for your children! And yet consulting a financial advisor or product provider for advice during the early stages of selection sometimes allows for the chance that you might only be advised of the products they offer or those that suit *their* bottom line better than yours.

Unless you go out with a sound understanding and a handful of suspicion, you might as well strip naked and write *rip me off, please* in red ink all over your body. So in this chapter I've brought together a summary of the most important features you need to know about when looking for reliable, conservative and easy to manage investment options for L-plate investors. You'll notice that means no mention of options, warrants or any other stockmarket product that requires a great deal of time, effort or skill to manage. At the other end of the scale, you'll also notice a handful of very common banking facilities that next to nobody ever thinks of as having investment benefits (usually because the product providers never advertise them that way).

CREDIT CARDS

Yes, credit cards! If you're shocked by the prospect of using them as an 'investment' vehicle for your kids' money, then you may not be thinking outside of your programming yet. Smack your fingers and consider that if you have a maxed-out credit card, your kids can loan you their savings to 'park' in your credit card account to reduce the amount of interest you pay. That way you'll owe money to your kids, not the bank, and you can pay them a lower rate of interest, saving you money and giving them some income that's higher than the interest from a normal savings account.

> **Warning:** Finances and family often make for an explosive mix and fights over money usually spread into squabbles over other things – and can damage relationships for a lifetime. So NEVER provide a loan to a family member unless you're on excellent terms to begin with AND you thoroughly trust each other, AND you work out a plan for repayments together AND you agree never to use the loan as a bargaining chip in future squabbles over other things.

CALCULATING DAILY INTEREST ON MONEY 'INVESTED' IN A CREDIT CARD

Interest on credit cards is calculated on a daily balance, so an easy-to-use formula that you can use to pay your children is based on a daily rate as follows:

> $ loaned to your credit card × interest rate ÷ 100 (to convert the interest rate to decimal) ÷ 365 (days in a year) = interest per day.

Then multiply the answer by the number of days that the child has the money 'parked' in the credit card account.

Handy hint: For more information about credit cards – and for a very handy free downloadable calculator to help you figure out the best repayments to help pay your credit card off the fastest – check out ASIC's website at www.asic.gov.au.

> **Student challenge: Investing in family credit cards**
> Work out how much you would earn in interest if:
> - You gave one of your parents $100 every fortnight for three fortnights to 'park' in their credit card.
> - From the fourth fortnight, you decide to invest your $100 somewhere else, but also ask your parent to keep the money that you've already invested for another 10 fortnights.
> - The credit card usually charges 17% and they agree to pay you 12% (saving themselves 5%).
> - They then keep the total loan in the credit card for the next 10 fortnights.
> - They pay you back in a lump sum (all at once) after a garage sale.
>
> For the answer, see Appendix 1: Handy hints for student challenges.

SAVINGS ACCOUNTS

Yes, these are definitely one of the most popular and easy options to arrange, but they can COST you money in many ways that very often render them even worse than keeping your money in a cookie jar (especially for small balances). For example:

- monthly fees and lower interest paid, which can send you backwards when you've only got a small amount (under $500) in your account;
- the hidden cost of not being able to earn high interest rates while you've got it sitting idle in your savings account.

The main problem to be aware of is to make sure the savings account you get has interest calculated on daily balances, instead of monthly balances and has low or no fees.

TERM DEPOSITS AND HIGH-INTEREST SAVINGS ACCOUNTS

As explained in 'A finance quiz' on page 119, by investing money in a term deposit you can earn more interest than if you left it in a high-interest-earning savings account – but not always, so be careful. If you choose a high-interest-earning savings account with no monthly fees, which deposits the interest into your account every month AND it's more often than the interest would be added to your term deposit, then you can end up earning more interest from the savings account, even if it looks as if the interest rate is a little bit lower. Term deposits pay you much better interest the longer your money is 'locked away' without having the interest deposited to your account. But if you open a term deposit with a slightly lower interest rate but one that 'rolls over' more often, you can end up with more interest in the long run.

> ### Definition alert!
> Interest 'rolls over' when it does the clever-doggie trick of rolling out of cyberspace into a bank account. Most banks give you a choice between letting your interest roll back into your term deposit where it can make your next interest payment higher OR rolling it out into any other bank account so you can spend it – but you have to decide BEFORE it rolls over.

OVERDRAFTS

Overdrafts are explained on page 128, so you should already understand how to use them. However, they're mentioned here again under the topic of investment opportunities to ensure you don't overlook the fact that they can earn reasonably good interest as soon as you've 'overpaid' the loan part of this account – at the same time as having the facility of a reasonably cheap emergency loan on standby (which I use for the purposes of buying shares from time to time when cash reserves are busy elsewhere). And since you have to make 'repayments' to your overdraft even when it owes you money, it can be a really great way of forcing you to save up for investments, as well as bills, special treats and holidays.

STOCKMARKET SHARES

Think carefully for a moment: Do you have an instant fear or aversion to the idea of investing in shares? If so, then be honest and ask yourself, are you:

1. Suffering a fear of the unknown? If so, this can be overcome cheaply and easily by having a go at this section.
2. Suffering once-burned-twice-shy syndrome, even when the first attempt you made was a random stab at a blue-chip or company that had been recommended to you without knowing how to double-check the figures and outlook properly for yourself? If so, then this chapter will help you discover why you went wrong.
3. Suffering from lack of confidence? Maybe you were no good at maths at school and therefore think you must be no good at investments that require a basic understanding of statistics and forecasts. But if you are ready to learn, then you can do it.
4. Suffering from programming by society, family or media to believe that only high-flyers, gamblers and risk-takers put their money into shares? The basics of profitable share investments are simple enough for high school students to learn – and talk about *fun*!

> **Don't let your financial future be ruled by fear. Learn first, then do – or don't do – based on goals and informed personal preferences.**

To help you where shares are concerned, here's a super-condensed overview of the things I've learned to look for in order to find conservative reliable shares on the Aussie stockmarket – investments that not only pay reasonably generous dividends at relatively low risk but also provide relatively high growth potential.

Did you know?

There are no expensive 'secrets' here. I simply researched using only free information sources, such as libraries, newspapers and various ASX handouts and websites. I then tested the steps for a year and have used them religiously for almost 10 years as follows:

Minimum conservative goals:

* Dividend income: 6% per year (after tax)
* Capital growth: 12% per year (before tax).

But, in practice, I'm happy to say that my total annual returns over the last 10 years have been over 8% from dividends and over 40% for capital growth.

THINGS YOU NEED:

* a copy of today's *Australian Financial Review*, plus one from last week/month if you can find it;
* a ruler to help read across lines of small print;
* a pen and two blank pieces of paper (one for your shortlist and one for scribbling notes);
* a calculator. It doesn't have to be scientific or financial: a basic model will do;
* online access to the free website of the Australian Stock Exchange (ASX) at www.asx.com.au will be helpful too, because you can enter the ASX code for each company (as listed in the market reports toward the back of the *Financial Review*) into the search engine to find handy info and charts about how each of your shortlisted companies is performing right up to the last few minutes or close of trading for the day.

10 EASY STEPS

1. Practise the next nine steps for three months with 'virtual money' so you get the hang of things without risking any real cash. Have fun doing it during lunch breaks at work or home with your teenagers and you'll soon discover whether investing in shares is the thing for you.

2. Draw up a page of columns like this:

Company	Div %	Franking Code	$ Last sale	52 week high	52 week low	P/E Ratio	EPS	What do they do?	Shareholder Discount?	Notes
E.g. Caltex	1	f	2.29	3.30	1.75	5.7	40	Fuel	No, sadly	

3. Open the *Financial Review* to the market reports labelled 'Industrials' for industrial stocks and run your finger down the dividend yield column on each page, looking for numbers between 7 and 12 which – very basically – mean that this is the approximate percentage rate of dividend you'll be paid, based on that day's purchase price, the amount of the last dividend that was paid to investors and the assumption that the company will be able to continue paying that level of dividend in future. It's the rough equivalent of choosing a term deposit that pays somewhere between 7% and 12% interest a year. For the resource stocks, which are further back in the newspaper and notoriously less likely to be focused on returning profits to shareholders, try looking for yields between 4% and 7%, noting that the per cent sign will be missing when you look down any of these dividend yield columns.

Also look for an 'f' in this column (or in the nearby column for $dividends) which means the dividend is fully franked (has had 30% tax already paid to the Tax Office so you can include it with your annual tax return too). A 'p' means that the dividend is partially franked and shares with no 'f' or 'p' means that you still have to pay tax on the dividend, just as you would for interest that you earn on your savings accounts at the end of each financial year. Use your ruler to help glance across the columns to the 52-week highs and lows to see how much the share price for this company has fluctuated in the last year. If it has obviously bounced back from its all-time low for the year and is still rising (which you can tell by comparing market reports a few weeks apart, from the graph of stats for that company on the ASX website or by speaking to your stockbroker), then simply compare the current share price and against the 52-week high to see how far it's likely to rise, assuming that the company is over the problems that made its share price fall.

Did you know?

By the end of step 3 (having completed steps 4 to 7 until you run out of companies) your shortlist usually contains between 5 and 25 opportunities for earning high income as well as potentially high growth in the short to medium term.

---

4. Look for shares priced under $10 each. There's nothing wrong with buying shares that are worth as much as $30 each or more, but if you buy a share worth $2.90, then every time it goes up by a cent, it will grow in value by .34482%, while a $29 share will only grow in value by 0.034482%.

5. Compare the NTA (Net Tangible Assets) column against the column with the current share price. If a share price is close to the value of its NTA, then it's likely (although arguable) that you're buying the share close to it's true value, rather than at inflated prices which fluctuate according to the whims of the company's goals.

6. Look for companies with a P/E (price compared to earnings) ratio between 6 and 14. Again, there are plenty of great investment opportunities outside my favourite suggested ranges, while many resource stocks don't report P/E ratios

at all. Generally speaking, a P/E ratio less than 6 means the company is either due for a bounce back and/or likely to bounce back slowly, while a P/E ratio over 14 means the share is beginning to get a little overpriced, usually on the basis of popularity or an expectation that the company is going to perform better in future.

7. Glance at the EPS (earnings per share). The higher the EPS the higher the profits the company is making. An EPS of 30, for instance, is usually extremely healthy. But if the EPS is negative then the company is making losses instead of profits, so an investment in a company of that kind is arguably very risky indeed.

8. Seek further info by:

   a. Calling your stockbroker to work through your final shortlisting process by asking questions like:
      • Which of my short-listed companies pay their dividends as DRPs (dividend reinvestment plans, which allot investors with more shares in the company instead of depositing a cash payment into their bank account)? With DRPs the investment continues to grow on top of itself, instead of flowing out where the benefits are easy to spend by accident.
      • Have you heard any recent reports that may effect the future earnings of each company? Which of my short-listed companies have reputations for paying strong dividends, even through harsh economic downturns?

   b. Searching the Internet for relevant helpful info, specifically seeking out:
      • the websites for each of your shortlisted companies where you can usually request a free copy of their most recent annual report, find out what they do and what their goals are;
      • the Australian Stock Exchange (www.asx.asn.au), where you can check out stacks of free info including company reports, latest sales statistics, graphs and media announcements;

- the Australian Securities and Investments Commission (www.fido.asic.gov.au), where you can find a range of warnings, handy tips and free info about investing (not only in shares);
- the Reserve Bank of Australia (www.rba.gov.au), which has some fantastic general information in their educational links (as well as a school-visit service!);
- the Australian Shareholders Association (www.asa.asn.au), which has a good smattering of consumer info outside their restricted members-only areas which can help L-plate investors even before they're ready to take that initial plunge.

Did you know?
By the end of step 8 the best three to five opportunities should be screaming at you from your shortlist.

---

9. Choose the price range you're prepared to pay for your shares by discussing the current (as well as recent and possible future values) with your stockbroker and/or using the 'course of sales' section at the back of the *Financial Review* to see the lowest and highest prices that have been paid on the previous day for your chosen company. Your stockbroker will also be able to discuss recent price fluctuations and trends with you during the course of a reasonably short phone conversation, provided that you have your shortlist down to three to five companies by this stage and you don't make a habit of pestering them regularly with phone calls that don't result in a buy/sell order.
10. Give your stockbroker clear instructions on which shares you'd like to buy, what prices you're prepared to pay and the total budget you've set aside to cover shares, stamp duty and broker fees (called brokerage). Then sit back and wait up to a week for it to happen, remembering that you will only have three working days to send the money to your stockbroker's account after the sale happens.

For thorough yet easy-to-follow details of the methods I use to sort good-value, reliable investments from the big-talking dog-investments, see the last chapter of *Your Money: Starting Out and Starting Over.* Or for the core information and favourite shortcuts that I started with during my first investments in shares and property, check out my two pocket books, *Your Sharemarket Jargon* and *Your Real Estate Jargon,* both of which contain more than just alphabetical listings of the most important terminology. (See also 'Sample share performances' on page 24.)

INVESTMENT PROPERTY

Owning investment properties with your parents can be complicated and financially messy – not to mention frustrating with a capital F – because while you get to share in some of the tax refunds every year (as well as some of the risk), your parents usually make all the decisions and it can be extremely hard to sell up and get your money out if you become desperate to escape the stress. On the other hand, many families get ahead financially faster by joint co-operation, for example, by buying a unit closer to a suitable university while your child is still young and using it as an investment property with the aim of owning it debt-free by the time your child is ready to move in and take advantage of much closer commuting distances. At the same time they'll develop the skills of renting or caring for a unit, but with the reassurance of considerate 'landlords' and parental help close at hand if needed.

Another way means living rent free – or practically rent free – at the same time as investing. This is especially effective where young-adult siblings with high disposable incomes have enough money for either: (a) a deposit on a house or unit, but can't afford to keep up repayments without tax breaks, or (b) can afford the purchase and repayments on a negatively geared investment property, but either can't afford to rent a place for themselves at the same time, or can't handle the stress of worrying if tenants are going to trash the place. So one solution is to have two siblings buy an investment property each and rent to each other, whether it's on opposite sides of the street or opposite sides of the country. All rent has to be swapped at market rates suitable for each property of course – and it's forbidden by law to negatively gear the house or unit that you live in as your permanent residence. Neither party would be eligible for the First Home Buyer's Grant, but would benefit every year from refunds of tax taken from their pay packets to compensate for their loan and management expenses.

INVESTMENT PACKAGING

This is a technical term that simply means choosing a few investments options which not only work well for your own personality type and situation, but also work well together. For instance, if you're the type of 'control freak' (like me!) who likes investments in which you can closely control expenses and ongoing management, then investment properties, term deposits and self-managed shares could be the way to go.

But if you're the type of personality who couldn't be bothered with 'all that investment stuff' then a reputable array of managed funds are probably the choice for you.

SUPERANNUATION

The following discussion is the barest bones of what super is and how it relates to your children and their first incomes. But the rules are complicated, so for more info contact the Australian Tax Office.

WHO'S ELIGIBLE?

Most working Aussies are covered by the Superannuation (super) Guarantee Charge, which means that every month their employers have to stash away at least 9% of each employee's pay as super savings. People who don't have the super stashed away by their employers can include:

- people over 70 years old;
- staff who get paid less than $450 per month;

- staff under 18 years of age (or employed for domestic or private work) and working 30 hours a week or less.

WHEN CAN YOU GET YOUR SUPER BACK?

Usually only when you permanently retire from the workforce, but sometimes super can be paid out early in cases of genuine and severe financial hardship, compassionate grounds or permanent incapacity to work.

If your date of birth is:	Then your minimum age for taking all your employer's superannuation benefits out is:
After June 1964	60
July 1963 – June 1964	59
July 1962 – June 1963	58
July 1961 – June 1962	57
July 1960 – June 1961	56
Before July 1960	55

Note: It is possible to return to the workforce after retiring, but job opportunities are usually limited. Some restrictions also apply to the amount of income from part-time work you're able to earn after retiring before it affects your pension from either Centrelink or your superannuation fund.

CAN I SWITCH MY SUPER FUND?

With the introduction of 'Super Choice' from 1 July 2005, employees now have greater decision-making control over which superannuation fund best suits their needs, also opening the way for super-fund managers to compete harder for our consumer investment dollars and hopefully pick up their game with more cost effective returns! But just because you can

---

Did you know?

A company that collects and invests your compulsory superannuation contributions from your employer as well as any voluntary contributions from you and/or any employer-enforced contributions from you, is called an RSA provider – someone who 'provides' your Retirement Savings Account.

---

switch, doesn't necessarily mean that you should. Compare schemes carefully, looking specifically at comparisons of their:

- earning rates before management fees;
- management costs;
- contribution fees;
- insurance fees per year;
- advisor service fees;
- forecast earnings for the coming year (and if they look too good to be true, it very well can often be an overestimation in the hope of attracting your investment dollars);
- termination costs, because you may decide to leave the new fund in a few years' time and you don't want to shift to a new fund if they're going to have unreasonable exit fees.

Talk to your existing fund's financial advisor if you don't trust your own figures, comparing what that fund has to say with what the new fund has to say (knowing they're both going to be biased towards their own products). And if you'd like any extra independent assistance, then speak to your bank's financial advisor or try using the free downloadable superannuation calculator now available on ASIC's website.

CAN I TOP UP MY SUPER?

Tax concessions sometimes make the option of topping up your superannuation out of your own pocket quite attractive, but you really have to weigh up whether you could put the money to better work elsewhere, perhaps by saving up for a car or home and then concentrating on paying them off – especially when you're at the start of your working life or have more than 10 years to go until retirement.

Up until age 65, members can contribute voluntary cash into their super accounts whenever they like. You have to be able to spare the money, of course, because once it goes in, it's not coming out for a long time (with a few very strict exceptions).Your super fund claims tax concessions, so the bottom line is a slightly better return than a similar outside investment that has to pay a higher rate of tax. Some companies also encourage their employees to put more into their super funds by offering to put more in too, if they do. After the age of 65 different rules apply, so if your existing fund doesn't let you make extra voluntary repayments after age 65, then consider using the ASIC calculator to see if it's worth changing to another fund.

If you're an employee who makes after-tax contributions and your total income is $28,000 or less, remember you may also receive a government co-contribution of $1.50 for every $1 you contribute (up to a maximum of $1500 from the government). You don't have to worry about claiming this. If you're eligible, your fund sends the information to the Tax Office and they pay it into your fund for you.

Sometimes employers allow you to make extra payments into super by reducing the amount of gross (pre-tax) income you get paid each week or fortnight. This is known as 'salary sacrificing' and it works best if your annual income is over $70,000.

It's also possible to pay super contributions on behalf of a non-working or less-working spouse or partner in order to get additional tax benefits.

While most people use a professional super fund, there is also DIY Super (Do-It-Yourself superannuation), also known as SMSF (Self-Managed Super Fund) or SMS (meaning Self Managed Superannuation). You have to make sure that your tax accountant is specially licensed to give you advice about setting up a self-managed super fund, because accountants who don't have an Australian Financial Services Licence are only allowed to provide advice about the establishment, operation, structuring and valuation of a DIY Super fund, not investment strategies or whether you should switch your existing super savings over to one. Errors, paperwork and legislation changes can be major hassles in managing your own super, and just because you're allowed to manage the money for your own future, DOESN'T mean that you're allowed to withdraw any for your own use before retirement.

FAMILY TRUSTS

A family trust is a legal entity created to pool and manage investment income, capital gains tax and expenses in a tax-effective manner while protecting assets against litigation and then distributing profits to the designated family members who are beneficiaries. But beware: distributions to children under 18 years of age will attract 66% tax (as explained on page 58) for any income over $417 in that financial year. Family trusts are best set up by a highly experienced, registered financial advisor and tax accountant. The laws regarding family trusts are often changed by newly elected federal governments, so even though you may spend time and money setting up a viable and tax-effective family trust, that doesn't mean that it will survive or thrive under future governments.

14

Other Programs, Initiatives, Resources and Opportunities

As part of its report for the ASIC discussion paper on Financial Literacy in Schools, Erebus Consulting Partners documented a range of existing programs and resources. These included:

- **Dollarsmart**, a resource for schools in the form of a workbook on CD, produced by the Financial Planners' Association's taskforce into financial literacy in schools. It is available as a free pdf download from www.fpa.asn.au.

- **Operation Financial Literacy**, an all-state pilot program run by Financial Basics Foundation – a not-for-profit organisation – with initial pilot programs in schools across Victoria, Queensland and Tasmania. Schools are provided with $3000 grants for projects which expose students in grades 8, 9 and 10 to topics such as managing credit, the importance of savings and the consequences of gambling. It's helpful in the long term because the grants aim to aid schools in developing independent resources to help themselves. Schools can apply to receive a grant at www.financialbasics.org.au.

- **Axiss Australia** – a government agency assigned to positioning Australia as a global finance centre in the Asian time zone – offers a series of work experience scholarships for school and uni students to engage in workplace learning in the financial sector. Launched initially in Perth, see their website, www.financescholars.com.

- **Finance First** is a NSW-based joint financial education project between the YWCA (Young Womens' Christian

Association) and Citigroup that aims to target adults and children simultaneously through selected primary schools. The project's *MakingCents* program aims to help parents teach children about money. It is soon to be expanded across all states in order to provide new curriculum course material for kindergarten to grade 6 (K-6). Website: www. ywca-sydney. com.au.

- **My Money My Future** is an Anglicare Tasmania project with funding from the Connect Community Foundation, the aim of which is to empower young people with the skills and knowledge to control their own finances. Website: www.anglicare-tas.org.au/services/mymoney.html.

Of course many other corporate, government and community groups have been attempting to support financial literacy for youth and families through a wide range of tightly focused opportunities for almost a century. The Commonwealth Bank has run one of the longest financial literacy promotional programs in the form of the school banking program with staff assigned to school visitations since the early 1930s! The Australian Stock Exchange (ASX, www.asx.com.au), Real Estate Institute of Australia (REI, www.reiaustralia. com.au) and Australian Securities and Investment Commission (ASIC, www.asic.gov.au), have also supported extensive free and highly valuable financial information for consumers for many years.

Since publication of ASIC's discussion paper in 2003, a number of new and existing programs, facilities and resources have been implemented or redeveloped, some of the most notable of which include:

- **Dollars and Sense** is an initiative sponsored primarily by the Commonwealth Bank (www.dollarsandsense.com.au) that provides online information tools and links to improve teen financial literacy in a very easy-to-read format. Ideal for free exploration by secondary students, but also highly suited to upper primary class groups progressing through each link under instruction by a parent or teacher, this website is definitely student-friendly – easy to use, understand and navigate.

- *MoneyMinded* is a program developed by the ANZ bank in association with the Centre for Learning Innovation (a sub-department of the NSW Department of Education) and also involving representatives from the Australian Financial Counselling and Credit Reform Association as well as ASIC. Launched in late 2004, it is an absolutely amazing free download resource centre designed to help teachers and workshop providers teach people to make better decisions about the use and management of their money. The initiative is not a sales-pitched exercise so there's no hard-sell of branded banking products. The *MoneyMinded* initiative aims to partner with 100 community organisations during the next five years to deliver financial literacy material to 100,000 people nationally, with free course material available for teachers and website facilitators online at www.moneyminded.com.au.

- **Financial First Steps** is an interactive workshop funded by Westpac Bank which is currently being developed to cover a range of basic money management topics. Website: www.westpac.com.au/internet/publish.nsf/Content/wiwcan +Financial+literacy.

- *To the Max* and *Moola Talk* are financial comic strips published by ASIC for all children aged 14 to 18 and specifically for Indigenous youth aged 10 to 16. They are available in hardcopy (ph. 1300 300 630) or on their website: http://www.fido.asic.gov.au/fido/fido.nsf/byheadline/ Moola+talk.

- **www.moneymanagement.com.au** is a free information website provided by Reed Business Information, a publisher of many business-related magazines. Although archived articles are predominantly for adults, the site provides a wealth of articles and information relevant to families and teenagers.

- **The Commonwealth Bank Foundation Financial Literacy Grants** in 2004 offered 100 grants of $3500 each to secondary schools nationally to help implement educational programs to develop student financial literacy awareness, understanding and skills. Each year the foundation also aims to offer 70 e-Learning Grants of $5000 each to primary schools across Australia in association with the Australian government's National Literacy and Numeracy Week. Website: www.commbank.com.au/foundation.
- **Regional Workshops** are offered in each state and territory by the Commonwealth Bank Foundation and the Enterprise Network for Young Australians (ENYA) to deliver money-management skills and financial information to regional young people aged 16 and over who are either working or engaged in tertiary education. ENYA offers free membership for young people and mentors and aims to help young adults learn financial and business skills to establish themselves in the business or community sectors. Website: www.enya.org.au.
- **Girl$avvy** is a series of one-day workshops offered every year by the NSW Premier's Office for Women for female high school students. It's aimed at motivating and educating young women about the importance of being financially aware. Website: http://www.women.nsw.gov.au/Working/Working_YoungW_girlSavvy.htm.
- **Saver Plus** is one of the most amazing pilot programs I've seen. Initiated by the ANZ bank, it aims to teach low-income families to save by paying them $2 for every $1 they save into a bank account (up to a maximum of $2000 per participant) and has already committed over $1.5 million to the project. The first *Saver Plus* pilot finished in February 2005 with 257 families in Victoria and New South Wales all saving towards their children's education. In addition to helping participants build confidence, a savings habit and gain financial knowledge, participants also reported increased self-esteem, better family unity and support

networks as well as a greater sense of control over the future. And even greater news for 400 more families, is the return and expansion of the program in 2006 with $1 million already set aside by ANZ to help struggling families. Website: www.anz.com/aus/aboutanz/Community/Programs/Saver.asp.

15

The Game Zone

This chapter provides a cross-section of financial fun for toddlers to teenagers, including:
- my favourite money-related games, which help to develop hands-on cash skills for various ages;
- maths puzzle stories to help encourage creative problem-solving skills;
- fractured financial fiction as bedtime stories to feed dreams with goal setting themes and raise opportunities to discuss financial topics with children who've outgrown fairy tales.

These games and stories provide parents with opportunities to provoke creative-thinking techniques and open minds to differing points of view on various aspects of finances.

COIN GAMES
FOR TODDLERS TO GRADE 1 (AGES 2 TO 6)
As soon as they're old enough to talk, they're old enough for this game. Use gold coins and large silver coins like tens, twentys and fiftys to see who in your family can spin each coin denomination the longest. Aside from gaining early coin recognition skills, this game also gives parents an opportunity to reinforce the hands-on skills of hygiene with money, ensuring that children understand the importance of washing hands after touching money and never ever putting it in their mouths.

During the early stages, your child will usually assume that bigger coins are worth more than small coins. This is why many plastic educational coin sets often size their faux coins with the smallest-value coins being the physically smallest and larger-value

coins being represented as physically larger, instead of repro-
duced in their accurate proportions. But I've found that
teaching with the real coins is helpful because you can pay
young children with a large silver coin (like a fifty cent piece) or
several tiny coins (like five cent pieces) to reward them for
attempts at completing their chores, while paying older children with more valuable but smaller gold coins.

But this isn't meant to 'cheat' the younger children out of
money, especially if it's a personal priority to ensure that you
treat your children equally, because often you'll get bigger
smiles by giving them a larger number of smaller coins, than
you will by giving them one valuable coin.

You could also invest the difference into a savings account
for the youngsters and in the process reduce the risk of the
valuable coins getting lost or flushed down the toilet! I've found
it's the principle of more work for more pay that is most helpful
– and it allows you the opportunity of letting them in on the
'secret' true values of money later on when they're learning
how to count up to 10.

Did you know?

One of the biggest complaints from employers about the
current and previous generation of school leavers, is their
inability to count change out to a customer without making
costly mistakes.

At the same time, I regularly witness cash transactions
where customers are given incorrect change between $0.05
and $10, and if I didn't mention it, they'd leave without
noticing.

**COIN GAMES FOR THE WHOLE FAMILY OR CLASS OF
STUDENTS**

The three games in the following student challenge – suitable
for ages six to 16 – are best played with a parent on pocket-

money payday in order to 'win' bonus pocket money. But they can also be played in a classroom environment to win (with the teacher's approval) a 'leave for lunch early' pass or 'get out of homework free' permit.

The games help teach a greater ability to see, feel and count small change instantly, which encourages the good habit of checking all change during cash transactions.

Game 1: Guess the dropped coin

Gather your siblings/classmates into a room where there's a hard smooth surface like floor tiles, timber or lino. (Be careful there are no cracks in the floor.) Blindfold everyone except your parent/teacher and ask them to assume the role of 'banker' to drop various coins – one for each denomination – at least three times from the same height onto the floor, announcing each one as it drops, until the players are used to the sound that each coin makes. Then the banker drops coins randomly to see if the players can tell which coin is dropped each time and keeps a scorecard of the ones that each player gets right. At the end of each round the scores are added up to see who wins. Advanced players can try using different and more challenging surfaces, like carpet, paving or bare concrete.

Game 2: Guess the coin in the dark

Similar rules to the game above, except you take turns recognising coins by touch while blindfolded. First get to know the feel of the coins without your blindfold, then with your blindfold on, guess the denomination of each coin that's put into your hand by the banker and add the values of correct coins to your score. Incorrect coins receive a score of zero. Repeat this three times each for each player. Finally, each try to draw the most valuable and least valuable coins out of the bag with your eyes closed. If you get them right, add the values to your score. But if you get them wrong deduct the values to reach your total score.

Game 3: Correct change

If parents regularly ask their kids if they can swap dollars for coins from their wallet with money that's all ready been handed out, sometimes deliberately give the wrong change. If the kids double-check their change without being reminded to, give them a 50-cent bonus. If they can tell how much the error is within a minute, give them a $1 bonus. If they can tell within a few seconds, give them a $2 bonus and if they're honest enough to notice that you've given them too much money AND give it back to you without being prompted, give them a $5 bonus. Why? Because some people can lose their jobs for honest mistakes and your child may be that unlucky person one day.

ON THE SUBJECT OF COMPUTERISED FINANCE GAMES

There's quite a range of excellent games that can be played for free or very low cost at your local library. Most are suitable for ages 4 to 9, with the ones available for X-box, computer and/or playstation including: Jumpstart Kindergarten, Jumpstart Preschool.

Free online games and free downloadable games for PCs are also available through links on my website, or you can search for more by using the following keyword sets:

Crazy cars	Money island	Dollar reef	Cash cloud
Cocopops	Hondabike	NZ money4kids	

Note: Pokemon card games – despite the fact that they have nothing to do with finance – have intense levels of score-keeping which involve fast-paced practice at maths which all has to be done in children's heads, and it's really quite awesome to see their maths skills pick up so quickly with these.

PUZZLE STORIES

Here's some fun maths puzzles from my personal collection. These sample stories are included here because they feature either:

- topics about money,
- my 50 Fun Rules for Success, and/or
- examples of how creative writing and mathematics can be mixed to help stimulate creative thinking and problem-solving. .

They're designed as fun challenges for high school students, or they can be used as bedtime stories or math games to be played by adults with primary school children. The characters are drawn from my series of action thrillers for kids called *Kirby's Crusaders*. The novel versions do not contain puzzles like this, but they do involve problem solving themes by focusing on a team of luckless teenagers who are learning how to earn an income, manage a business and co-operate with each other in order to become goal achievers through a string of mad-cap adventures while still at high school.

KIRBY'S STICK PUZZLE

Kirby galloped her black horse, Fidget, deeper into the crusty forest.

'Faster, girl!' she cried. 'We have to find our missing calf before the wild dogs get it!' Kirby steered away from the direction her brother had taken to maximise the size of their search area, then she leapt her horse over a dry creek and galloped up the next hill.

'Woah!' she yelled, pulling hard on the reins. Fidget skidded to a stop and a cloud of dust rose around them. 'I see smoke! Down there by the lake,' she said, turning her horse to face it. A tall ribbon of blue smoke rose above the trees and Fidget snorted. 'Change of plans,' Kirby agreed. 'Fire in a dry forest like this could kill everything!'

Kirby and Fidget raced downhill to check it out. They burst through the clump of trees and found two boys sitting by a campfire.

'Are you crazy?' Kirby yelled. They turned around and she

recognised them as Lew and Creedy, two tough kids from the other side of the lake.

'Oh, it's you,' Creedy said. 'The rate you galloped in, we thought a stampede was coming.'

Kirby leapt off her horse and rushed toward the fire. 'Are you trying to kill yourself?' She kicked dirt over the flames. 'Don't you guys know that it's fire season? One spark in the grass and the whole valley would go up in flames!'

'You're breaking my heart,' Lew said. He scooped up another pile of branches. 'Now get away from our fire. We need it to put a brand on our calf.'

'What calf?' Kirby asked. Then she saw it tied up on the ground. She dodged past Lew and kicked the last flicker of flames out.

'Hey!' Creedy whined. 'What did you do that for?'

'That's our calf!' Kirby said. She headed over to let it go. 'It escaped through the fence and my brother and I have spent hours trying to find it.'

'It's ours now,' Lew said. 'It didn't have a brand on it, so it must be wild.'

No point in arguing, Kirby thought. Her mind raced to think of a solution. Both boys were bigger than her. She couldn't fight them and she knew that she couldn't gallop home to get help or they'd be gone with the calf by the time she got back. Then she remembered the two rules of business that she'd been learning at school that week: defeat your corporate enemy with strategy, not fighting, and exploit your strengths at the same time as your competitor's weaknesses.

Kirby saw the bundle of sticks in Lew's hands and knew what she had to do.

'I'll make a deal with you,' she said. 'Let me arrange those sticks into a simple maths puzzle and if you can solve it in less than five minutes, then you get to keep the calf and I won't tell the police or the forest department that you were in here lighting fires – so long as you don't light any more. And if you can't solve it, you have to give me the calf and I'll give you a head start before sending the authorities after you.'

Lew scratched his head. 'Sounds too easy!'

'I'm game,' Creedy agreed. 'It will be a pleasure watching you lose!'

Kirby smiled, thinking exactly the same thing. She laid the seven sticks down on the ground like a math sum written with roman numerals.

$$X - I = I$$

'Ten minus one does not equal one,' she said. 'But you only have to move one stick to make it correct. And I'll even be generous and give you five minutes each to solve it.'

'It can't be solved,' cursed the two cow thieves at the end of ten minutes. 'We dare you to solve it right now, or else we get to keep your horse as well as the calf!'

'No problem,' Kirby said. She moved one stick and the boys were so impressed they even helped her to put the calf up onto her horse.

Which stick did Kirby move?

(Please turn to page 226 to see the answer. And no cheating! This one is really cool for stimulating your creative thinking!)

KIRBY'S CHAT ROOM PUZZLE

Kirby logged on to the computer at school and met her cousin, Scott, in the interschool chat room.

'Hey, Kirby!' he typed onto her screen from the other side of the mountain range. 'I found a really cool maths puzzle for you!'

'Give up, Scott!' Kirby laughed as she typed her reply onto the screen. 'You'll never beat me.'

'That's what's so fantastic about this puzzle, Kirby. I don't have to beat you! It's against the clock, so you'll be racing yourself.'

'Okay, now you've intrigued me,' Kirby said. 'Send it over.'

'There are rules,' Scott warned. 'You can't use a calculator and you have to finish it by 5 pm. Are you game?'

'Quit stalling,' Kirby answered as she glanced at the antique cuckoo clock on the wall. 'It's half past four now. Send it over!'

Kirby's inbox chimed a few seconds later and she opened the attachment, which read: Add one straight line to make the statement correct:

$$20 \ 10 \ 5 = 4.40$$

'Tick tock . . . tick, tock' Scott typed into the chat-room. 'Give up, Kirby,' he teased. 'You'll never get it in time!'

'Not with you bugging me every two seconds,' Kirby replied. She stared at the problem on her screen, then glanced to the clock and back to the problem again.

'Got it!' she said, typing the answer underneath the problem and emailing the file back to him. 'That was a good one!'

'Show off!' Scott teased. 'What gave it away so quickly?'

'You did.' Kirby typed a long row of smiley faces into the chat room. 'It would have been much harder if you hadn't kept bugging me about the time!'

Can you solve the problem in less than half an hour too?

(Turn to page 226 to see the answer.)

FEEDING DREAMS WITH FRACTURED FINANCE TALES

Here are a handful of bedtime stories to help feed the dreams of your primary-school aged children. Each part of each story raises a number of financial topics for discussion with your children, as described at the end of each section.

STORY 1. GRANNY MACLEOD'S MAGIC MONEY TREE

(A not-so-tall-tale about the magic of compounding interest.)

Part One

Once upon a tomorrow, there lived a wise old grandmother called Granny MacLeod who lived on a small, bushy farm way out on the edge of town, where she spent her spare time breeding ostriches, emus, zebra finches and red chickens. One night, very close to midnight, Granny M was in her bedroom, whispering bedtime stories to her five cats and her favourite pet chicken, when she heard a wild screeching of tyres outside on the road, soon followed by the sound of two large bangs and more tyres screeching.

Granny M leapt to the front window, peeped through the curtains and saw a large picnic basket sitting on the garden path.

No dogs barked anywhere on the neighbouring farms and her birds all remained silent in their pens, so she put on her dressing gown and scurried out to find a small baby sound asleep inside the basket.

'Scotty!' she said, as she recognised the face of her tiniest grandson. 'Your parents are off on another mission, are they?'

The baby kept sleeping.

He could sleep through a nuclear bomb, thought Granny MacLeod, and as she lifted his basket and carried him toward the lights of the house, she noticed a tiny 'Thank you' card dangling from the handle. Inside it she saw a quickly scrawled password and a bank account number. At the bottom of the card, she also saw a short coded message explaining why his parents had to disappear for a long time.

Granny M frowned, glancing up and down the silent road one last time, but she couldn't see any sign of Scotty's parents so she hurried him inside. Then she waddled straight into her bedroom, pushed three of her cats off her bedside table and took a little pink laptop computer out of her bottom drawer, where she'd hidden it amongst her baggy cotton underwear. She switched it on – the computer, not the undies – plugged it into the phoneline beside her bed and logged on to the Internet.

A few buttons later, she discovered that the joint bank account number given to her by her daughter and son-in-law only had a current balance of $100.86. But from the previous six months worth of bank statements, she could also tell that the account had no monthly fees and was being topped up regularly by $220 that deposited every second Thursday from somewhere – or *somebody* – else.

Granny M scratched her hairy chin for a moment, then surfed around the Internet to compare interest rates on all the different types of bank accounts. And just as her favourite pet chicken, Beakface, hopped up onto her lap and she fluffed through his feathers, she realised that if she needed to look after her baby grandson for a few years, then she was going to have to plant a fast-growing money tree to help look after him in case anything happened to her as well.

'But where can I plant a money tree,' she muttered, 'so it will be safe and grow the fastest?' Then she remembered reading a chapter from a book called *Your Kids' Money* a long time ago – and she clicked her fingers as the idea struck her with a buzz of excitement.

She began by coding in rules into the bank accounts to make sure the whole $220 would be sucked out of the mystery bank account as fast as somebody else kept putting the money in. She wondered who the mystery person might be and where the $220 kept coming from. Perhaps it was her daughter or son-in-law depositing money from wherever in the world they happened to be. Or maybe it was part of their pay from the central spy network that her son-in-law worked for? On the other hand, it did look a lot like the payment that her daughter was supposed to get from the government department called Centrelink as an allowance to help her to stay home to look after her baby. But whoever it was, Granny M could only guess.

All she knew was that for as long as someone kept putting money into the mystery account, she'd have to take it out to help pay for things the baby needed, as well as add small bits to an extra bank account – a bit like adding money leaves to a tiny money tree to help it grow.

So Granny M made sure that $200 was spent every two weeks on living expenses for baby Scott – things like food, clothes, shoes and nappies.

Finance topics to raise for discussion:
- As an exercise in basic budgeting and planning, encourage

your child to think of anything else Granny M needs to buy to help care for a baby? Sample answers: medicine, baby bath, cot . . . and did you think of anything else?

- As an exercise in mental finance calculations for children who've started to learn about double-digit addition at school, ask your child the following question: If the mystery account gets $220 every fortnight, and Granny M spends $200 to care for the baby, how much is left to save up money leaves for the money tree?

- Then ask: Are you ready to go to sleep, yet? If not, keep reading . . .

GRANNY MACLEOD'S MAGIC MONEY TREE

The story so far: Granny M has to look after her baby grandson from now on, and has $220 being sent to her every two weeks through a mystery account to help her. She spends $200 to help look after baby Scott, then . . .

Part Two

Granny M arranged for the last $20 every two weeks to go from the mystery account into a special bank account called a savings account, which would pay her interest – more money, this time from the bank – as a reward for keeping the money in there. She also shifted $100 that was sitting in the mystery account into the savings account so nobody else with access to the account could take it unexpectedly. She called this new savings account 'Baby Scott's Magic Money Tree.'

Then she closed down her laptop computer, unhooked it from the phone line, stashed it away secretly into her bottom drawer full of baggy undies and went to bed for the night.

Tick tock, tick tock . . . Time passed, as time does. The weeks turned into months, the months turned into years and as Baby Scott grew, so did his secret little money-tree savings account.

At first the money tree earned only 5% interest per year – that's only $5 worth of free money from the bank as a reward for each $100 that Granny M put in there. But the interest payments from the bank went into the account a little bit every month – and worked like fertilizer, making the tiny money tree grow a little bit faster each time that Granny M could manage to put money into it by herself. And even at this relatively slow rate, Baby Scott's money tree was worth $1200 by the time he turned two years old!

But then Granny M double-checked her calculations again – using simple maths rules that she learned way back during her high-school days, and she worked out that if the money tree kept growing at the same rate of 5% a year, it would be worth $12,000 by the time Scott turned 16 years old! (Quite a bit of money considering it grew from little payments often, don't you think?)

'But it's not enough to look after Scott if anything bad happens to me!' muttered Granny M. She went down to her bird pens – her favourite place in the world when she needed to think – and as she shovelled out the latest layers of bird poo from the nesting rooms and emptied it onto her rose gardens to make the plants grow faster, she realised that Scott's money tree needed extra fertiliser too. She kicked the poo off her boots and hurried back into her bedroom, swiped the cats off her bedside table, pulled her secret laptop out of her undies drawer and logged back onto the Internet.

This time, she found a website for a stockbroker – a special professional devoted to helping people invest money into a thing called the sharemarket.

'Which . . .' explained the stockbroker, in his very clever sounding introduction on his website, 'is a bit like owning lots of little pieces of many different types of big companies that you couldn't afford to buy if you tried to buy the whole things by yourself. But if you invest *a little* bit into them, the companies grow in value AND they pay you dividends, which is a lot like the interest you earn on your savings account.'

'Goodie!' shouted Granny M as she clapped her hands together, and she used the information from the website to invest in shares of a company that planned to grow in value by

12% every year AND pay her at least 7%, when the savings account had only been paying her 5%.

More time passed, as time does, and by the time Baby Scott turned four, his secret money tree had grown to $2840! By the time he turned 10, it was $13,000! And on his 16th birthday, it was $42,200!

That's nearly FOUR TIMES what it would have been if she'd left the money tree sitting in the savings account, starving for more fertilizer.

By then Scott was a teenager who was earning his own part-time income by working at the local cafe after school, working hard to save up for a motorbike because he wanted to start cross-country racing.

Granny M shivered at the thought of him getting hurt, so she didn't tell him about the secret money tree account that could have paid for a brand new bike a few times (and still had change left over!). Instead she continued to let Scott save up for the motorbike by himself and left the money tree to keep growing in secret, so by the time Scott turned 21, his money tree had shot up past $100,000! (Note for parents: by this time, Granny M could have been making contributions to the money tree out of either her own pocket, her family tax benefit (A) and/or Scott's contributions for board and lodgings now that he has his own source of income to help contribute to house-hold living expenses.)

Granny M did her maths again and discovered a magical thing. She didn't have to put $20 into the money tree account ever again. It was now growing much faster than she could keep up with!

Finance topics to raise for discussion:
- Discuss how Granny M was putting in a total of 26 lots of $20 each year – and that only totals $520 per year. But by the end of the story, the growth of the investment is $20,000 a year AND . . . STILL . . . GROWING!
- Re-emphasise the magic of compound interest – money that

grows and grows on top of itself year after year – and point out how, by his 40th birthday, Scott would have nearly $4 MILLION!

- Encourage their excitement at the potential earnings and discuss any changes to goals for their own bank accounts, pocket money and saving strategies.

MAD MURPHY'S MISSING MOUNTAIN OF GOLD

A remix of one of my favourite old Aesop's fables about misers.

Part One

Kirby MacLeod and her cousin Scott crept through the dark shadowy scrub at the edge of her father's farm, watching Old Mad Murphy on the other side of the fence as he did strange things in the moonlight behind his rickety tractor-shed.

'What's he doing?' Scott asked as he crouched into the bushes beside her.

'He's digging another hole,' Kirby whispered. 'He's maaaaad! Totally mad! He goes back there every morning and every night and each time he digs that same enormous hole behind the shed. He stares into it for a while, then covers it over again and sneaks back to his house as if he's just buried a dead body!'

'Maybe it IS a dead body,' Scott snickered. 'With all the weird things that go on around this town, nothing surprises *me*, anymore.'

'It can't be anything like that,' Kirby said. 'He has *three* dogs, we have a dog and there are dingoes that come down from the hills every night. If there was anything dead over there, it wouldn't stay buried for long. They'd dig it up.'

'That's true,' Scotty whispered as he saw Old Mad Murphy sit down and make himself comfortable beside his hole. He set his shovel aside, crossed his legs and smiled as he stared down into his hole. 'His poor old mutts are so scrawny, they could smell dead meat a mile away.'

'It's a disgrace,' Kirby whispered. 'People should take better care of their pets than that – especially him. I heard that he's filthy rich, did you know that?'

'NO WAY!' Scotty slapped his hand over his own mouth, hoping Mad Murphy hadn't heard him. But the old man glanced up and looked nervously straight towards them. Then he grabbed his shovel and started filling the hole back in as fast as his old muscles could hussle.

'Uh-oh,' Scotty whispered. 'He's onto us.'

'I doubt it,' Kirby whispered. 'He's always jumpy like that. Half deaf in one ear. Last week, I saw him spook at a baby rabbit. A few days before that, it was a swarm of cabbage moths. And a few days before that, it was truck lights pointed his way from the other side of the lake. He only looks this way each time because the silly old fool thinks I'm always watching him.'

'But if you're not always watching him, then how do you know that he always looks this way when he thinks you're watching him?'

'Whose side are you on?' Kirby said, with a cheeky glare in Scott's direction.

'I have to be quiet now,' he answered.

They watched Mad Murphy for a few minutes longer until the skinny old farmer had turned the hole into a trampled hill. He jumped up and down all over the loose dirt like a kid on a lumpy brown trampoline.

'So what makes you think that's he's rich?' Scotty whispered as the old man hung his shovel onto the wall of the shed and headed back past his sleepy dogs toward his house. 'Look at him! He dresses like someone who lives in a rubbish bin! His house is a total wreck and his dogs are so scrawny the poor things are hardly bothering to lift their heads!'

'That's true,' Kirby said, 'and his poor cows and chickens aren't much better. A good thing they can survive on grass and breaking into his pumpkin patch every now and then, or else they would have died years ago!'

'So if he ever used to be rich, then he must have lost it.'

'Maybe,' Kirby said. 'The rumour is that he found a gold nugget years ago when he was ploughing his field. It was big, like the tip of a mountain, or so I heard, and reporters came from all over the world to take pictures. Then strangers flooded into the valley too and the rumour goes that one of them tried to steal it. Maybe one of them did, my dad said, because nobody's ever seen or heard of the nugget since . . .'

Kirby and Scott looked at each other. They glanced over to Old Mad Murphy's mound of dirt, then they looked back to each other again.

'Are you thinking what I'm thinking?' Scotty asked.

'Right behind you,' Kirby agreed. 'If he stashed a big lump of gold down there, he should be putting it to good use, instead of letting everything around him fall to waste! It's a total disgrace!'

'You don't mean that we're going to steal it?' Scott said, staying put. 'Mad Murphy may be a mean old miser man, but he still seems basically honest to me.'

'Not steal it,' Kirby said. 'Come on, Snotty-babe. I've got an idea that's just right for a pair of crusaders!'

'I hate it when you say that,' Scotty muttered and he dropped down to his belly to follow her underneath the fence. 'I always end up filthy!'

A few hours later, both of the teen crusaders had dirt from their eyebrows to their toenails.

'It's not as big as I expected,' Kirby said. 'About the same size as a pumpkin.'

Scotty groaned. 'I'm never going to dig another hole in my life!'

Kirby smiled as she glanced toward Murphy's scrawny dogs, lying sound asleep beside his pumpkin patch.

'Oh yes you are,' she giggled. 'Except the next hole doesn't have to be so deep.'

Finance topics to raise for discussion:
• Discuss the differences between Mad Murphy's method of

keeping his wealth safe against Granny MacLeod's choice of investing from the previous story.

- Compare Mad Murphy's method of savings to your child's method of keeping money in a piggy bank at home or putting it into a bank account to earn interest.
- Also discuss the purchase of goods that have no resale value as well as the purchase and maintenance of goods in order to keep or improve their value.
- Discuss the kinds of purchases that your child makes which have:
  ○ zero resale value, as in the case of food and entertainment such as movies and trips to theme parks,
  ○ partial resale value as in second-hand goods, toys or furniture, and
  ○ higher resale value, as in the case of second-hand furniture that's been restored or bargains purchased for less than your child could re-sell them.
- From a social and moral point of view, you could also discuss alternative action that Scott and Kirby could have taken. For example, discussing Mad Murphy's weird behavior with their father, reporting his suspicious behaviour to the police if they were really concerned, or just leaving the old guy alone, since he's not hurting anyone and taking the law into their own hands could lead them into big trouble, the first of which would be trespassing.
- Are you ready for sleep yet, sleepy heads, or do you want to read part two, to see what Kirby and her cousin Scott did?

MAD MURPHY'S MISSING MOUNTAIN OF GOLD

The story so far: Kirby and Scott noticed miserly Mad Murphy digging a hole behind his tractor-shed one night. Thinking he might be hiding a giant gold nugget while his farm animals are starving, they decide to teach him a lesson . . .

Part Two

A few minutes later they finished digging and filling their second hole.

'That's it, I'm dead!' Scotty moaned. 'My arms are dead, my back is dead. I never want to see another shovel again.'

'Deal,' Kirby said and she led the way home to wash the evidence of their deed from their hands.

'I sure hope he's got a good sense of humour,' Scotty warned.

'Well if he hasn't, he'll be able to afford one when he realises what we did . . .'

Tick . . . tock . . . tick . . . tock . . . The hands of the clock above Kirby's bed moved slowly through the night as if someone had clogged them full of jelly. Then as the small hand clicked on to five o'clock in the morning, they heard Mad Murphy's scream echo all the way across the valley, lake and back again.

'We slept in!' Kirby cried as she ran out into the lounge room where her cousin snored inside his one-man-tent. 'Wake up, cuz! Wake up! It's crusader time!'

She pulled him out by the sleeve and dragged him across the carpet until he scraped himself awake. 'Crikey, Snotty, you could sleep through an earthquake!'

It took another few minutes to shake the dreams out of Scotty's head, and as he peeled himself out of his sleeping bag, they heard the heavy thump of Mad Murphy's boots pounding up the back steps.

'KIRBY MACLEOD!' he shouted. 'YOU COME OUT HERE RIGHT NOW!'

Kirby brushed her long black hair out of her face and pushed her broad sweet smile out of the kitchen window, right beside him.

'Something wrong, Mister Murphy?'

'You know it is, girl!' he hissed at her like a spitting snake. 'Where is it? What did you do with it?'

'With what, Mister Murphy? And would you mind keeping your voice down? You'll wake the rest of the family.'

'My Go—' he said, stopping himself as soon as he saw Scott standing behind her. 'My gosh!' he said instead. 'You know exactly what I'm talking about! It was a big lump of rock about the same size as a pumpkin! And now it IS a pumpkin! See?' he pulled out a giant yellow pumpkin from behind his back, all dusty as if he'd only just dug it out from a deep hole. 'Look at that!' he ordered. 'Tell me, what do you have to confess about that?'

'Yep,' Kirby said, nodding toward the pumpkin, 'that's definitely a pumpkin.'

'Definitely a pumpkin,' Scotty agreed. He tried not to grin.

'Don't you try to be cute with me! I know you two had something to do with this! It wasn't a pumpkin yesterday, but it's certainly a pumpkin today!'

'Dear me, Mr Murphy,' Kirby said, shaking her head. 'You're not making very much sense. Would you like to come in for a nice hot cup of tea?'

Mad Murphy stamped his big yellow rubber boot. He shook the pumpkin like a ticking time bomb and his face turned red as if it was about to blow up too. Then he leaned closer to Kirby. 'I know you took my treasure,' he whispered, squeezing his words out hoarsely between his teeth as if trying to stop anyone else in the house from overhearing him.

Scotty leaned closer to make sure he didn't miss out.

'I check it every day and it's always there. And now it's not, but this is! This worthless, yellow bruised and battered pumpkin! I can't believe how worthless it is, I can't even sell it!'

'So how much is your treasure worth by comparison?' Kirby asked.

'Why, it's worth millions!' Mad Murphy answered, getting even grumpier. 'It's priceless, you silly girl. It's one in a kazillion! You could never afford it, that's for sure. I don't think anyone on the planet could have enough money to buy it from me! I'd never sell it anyway! It's mine, I tell you! I found it!'

'But you found that pumpkin too, Mister Murphy. And if you *can't* sell the pumpkin because it's worthless, and if you *won't* sell your treasure because it's priceless, then aren't they worth the same thing to your wallet and bank account?'

Mad Murphy stopped getting angrier and all the colour fell out of his face.

'That can't be right,' he squawked. 'Something that is price-less HAS to be worth more than something that's worthless.'

'Why?' Kirby asked, 'when you can bury that pumpkin back into the hole and dig it up again every day to make sure it's there, just the same as your treasure? How is it worth any different?'

Mad Murphy scratched his head in disbelief, wondering why he couldn't figure out how to answer Kirby's argument.

'And actually,' Kirby continued. 'Since you can scrape out the seeds and grow them to make more pumpkins, and then you can use those pumpkins to make even more pumpkins, after a while, you'll have enough pumpkins to bury as many as you want in holes in the ground AND have plenty left over to sell to buy food for your dogs AND fix your house AND even more to feed to your farm animals to help them grow fat and happy too. So doesn't that make the pumpkin in your hand far more useful and valuable than any-sized treasure that you could bury in a hole?'

Mad Murphy frowned and scratched his chin. 'I'm taking my pumpkin and going home now,' he said. 'It looks like I've got a full day of gardening ahead!'

Kirby smiled. 'Then make sure you dig over your pumpkin patch first!,' she called after him as he trudged down the steps. 'As my dad always says, good things come to those who sweat!'

'See?' she told Scott as soon as Murphy disappeared through the scrub toward the fence. 'Who said you can't teach an old dog new tricks?'

Scotty laughed. 'Do you think he'll bury the nugget again after he finds where we covered it in his pumpkin patch?'

'Who knows,' Kirby said. 'He's not called Mad Murphy for nothing. But at least from now on, his farm animals should be better fed!'

Finance topics to raise for discussion
- Discuss the two opposing points of view relating to some-thing that's purchased for long-term investment.
  a. Keeping it safe as an asset so it doesn't reduce in value, even if you know that it won't increase very much except by natural inflation. Explain how inflation is the natural increase in value of things over time and provide examples of how much toys and basic foods cost when you were a child as compared to their prices now. Now is also a good time to describe how such assets of high value can be used as 'security' by a bank to ensure that you'll repay a loan, or else the bank gets to keep the assets and all your repayments up until you 'default' on your loan – which means not paying as much in repayments as you're supposed to.
  b. The situation of buying something that you know you would never EVER sell, which could arguably be the same as making it worthless – at least until you die and leave it to somebody else as an inheritance in your will.

16

A Happy Ending

It's what every parent hopes and dreams is waiting ahead – up there in the distant future – for each of their children. Many even dream of the wealth coming to their family quickly and easily. But even if all your children win gold lotto, marry foreign royals or strike it rich with an inheritance from their estranged Great-Great-Aunt Winifred, it's just as likely they'll be unhappy if they haven't learned the character-building traits that financial literacy and proficiency can teach them along the way. Or worse, they could fritter away their wealth as quickly as it came to them, adding guilt, frustration and hopelessness onto their shoulders into the bargain.

It is so much more gratifying to stand on a firm mound of financial success – built step, rock and brick by yourself atop the foundations of love and guidance from your parents, wider family, friends and networking associates. And it is so much harder to knock such a well-reinforced mound of success out from beneath you!

Now here's your chance to make it possible for your own family. Simply get yourselves organised. Use the tools from this book to work it out for yourself and set the pace. Then teach the skills to your children by encouraging them as you lead the way with a fresh start and your own example. But enough from me! You're standing at the threshold of a long, but very exciting and adventurous path with your children and I'll bet you're just itching to get started. So here's a kiss for luck from me . . .

. . . and a pat on the back with this book in the hope that it helps to get you started (and re-started as often as you and the changing circumstances of your family need it!)

Anita B.

Appendix I

Hints for Student Challenges

Student challenge: Investing in family credit cards, page 180

Here's the question again, rearranged a little with hints added:

Use the formula on page 179 to work out how much Granny M would pay Scott in total (loan plus interest) assuming the credit card usually charges Granny 17% and she agrees to pay Scott 12% for the portion of money that he is able to provide to her as a loan. She's saving herself 5% on this amount of money, but this figure is not needed for your calculation. The other figure you don't really need to know is the total amount that Gran owes.

Scott gives her $100 every fortnight for three fortnights to 'park' in her credit card, so every fourteen days, the amount of his investment loan to her goes up by $100. This happens three times, so you'll need three short calculations to figure out the amount of interest for each set of fourteen days like this (rounded to nearest 4 decimals):

$100 loan × 0.12 interest ÷ 365 days in a year × 14 days = $0.4603
Plus $200 loan × 0.12 ÷ 365 days in a year × the next 14 days = $0.9205
Plus $300 loan × 0.12 ÷ 365 days in a year × the 3rd set of 14 days = $1.3808

Then at the end of the third fortnight, instead of getting an extra $100, she's told she can keep the total loan so far for the next 10 fortnights so add an extra ($300 × 0.12 ÷ 365 days in a year × 140 days) = $13.81.

So the total amount Gran pays Scott as a lump sum after selling her junk at a garage sale (in order to pay him without going back into debt on her credit card) is $316.60, which is made up of $300 + 0.4603 + 0.9205 + 1.3808 + 13.81 and rounded to the nearest five cents.

Conclusion: Scott's 'investment' in his Gran's credit card earned $16.57 interest rounded up to $16.60 for cash, which Gran was able to pay to him because she didn't have to pay $25.43 to the bank during this time and was therefore still better off by $8.83 (before rounding)!

But if Scott had invested in a savings account (for example one that's earning about 6% per year and calculates interest daily) he would have earned about $9.07 instead (minus any amount for a monthly account fee and with small variations depending on what day of the month interest is calculated into the account as well as how far into the first month Scott originally opens his account and makes the first deposit).

Note for advanced students: The calculation for working out interest in a savings account under these circumstances is a LOT more complicated, but for any advanced students who want to work out how to do it, the assumptions and calculations I used for the above example are that Scott used a savings account that calculates interest daily but deposits it into his account at the end of each month. The best rate he found was 6% and there are 11 days to go to the end of the month after his second instalment.

Therefore the calculation goes like this:

Loan at the beginning of the month = 0, so interest for 1st part of month = 0

Plus $100 × 0.06 ÷ 365 days in a year × 14 days = $0.2301
Plus $200 × 0.06 ÷ 365 days in a year × 11 days = $0.3616

Then monthly interest deposits to his saving account bringing the total investment to **$200.59** (note: the bank usually rounds down to the nearest cent when making the deposit). And there's now only 3 days to go until his next deposit, so the next batch of interest will be:

Plus $200.59 × 0.06 ÷ 365 days in a year × 3 days in the fort-night = $0.0989

(Which is still hanging in bank cyberspace at the time Scott adds his third batch of $100.)

Then after he makes his deposit, the next fortnight worth of interest is

Plus **$300.59** × 0.06 ÷ 365 days in a year × 14 days = $0.6918

Then assuming it's a 31 day month, there'll be exactly 14 days left to the end of the month (3 + 14 + 14 = 31), so interest for the first of the extra 10 fortnights will be

Plus **$300.59** × 0.06 ÷ 365 days in a year × 14 days = $0.6918 (as well)

Then interest will be deposited out of bank-cyberspace into Scott's account, so the opening balance at the start of the next month is: $302.07 (assuming the bank rounds down to the nearest cent or $302.08 if they round up).

Now we have 9 more fortnights to calculate interest for, so for the sake of this example, I assumed the next few months all have 30 days, but when working it out exactly for a real situation with exact dates, you'd be able to use a calendar to work out exactly how many days worth of interest you have to calculate each month by looking at the calendar and physically counting them (and replacing the number 30 in the following calculations with the right number).

The next month (2 fortnights, plus 2 days) worth of interest would be:

$302.08 × 0.06 ÷ 365 days in a year × 30 days = 1.4897, bringing the account balance to $303.56.

The next month (2 fortnights, plus 2 days) worth of interest would be:

$303.56 × 0.06 ÷ 365 days in a year × 30 days = 1.4970 bringing the account balance to $305.05.

The next month (2 fortnights, plus 2 days) worth of interest would be:

$305.05 × 0.06 ÷ 365 days in a year × 30 days = 1.5043 bringing the account balance to $306.55.

So far, we've worked out what 6.428 extra fortnights are worth, but we still have 3 fortnights and 8 days to go as follows:
The next month (2 fortnights, plus 2 days) worth of interest would be:

$306.55 × 0.06 ÷ 365 days in a year × 30 days = 1.5117 bringing the account balance to $308.06.

The next month (1 fortnight, plus 6 days) worth of interest would be:

$308.06 × 0.06 ÷ 365 days in a year × 20 days = 1.01 bringing the CLOSING account balance to $309.07 about half way through the month when he takes all his money out.

So Scott's total interest earned for the savings account which calculates interest on a daily balance would be about: $9.07.

Student challenge 2: role models, page 152

Use a large sheet of project paper, a notebook or the notes pages in the back of your school diary (if allowed) to draw up a table of role models (or anti-role models) as shown below – one table for each role model. I've filled out this one with an example of one of my role models, my dad.

My father	Really good at keeping his cool during an argument

Why it's important to me: I used to cave in during arguments with people who are really hot tempered, but he showed me excellent examples of how to keep my cool and argue my case (as fairly as possible) in order to stop the problem from getting worse.

For example: A really aggressive neighbour came over one day to argue with him about putting up a new fence between our properties. We wanted a new fence between us too. The bigger the better, I thought! And we had to share the expenses 50:50. But this guy wanted to force us to choose his mate to do the work for a really rip-off price, so we'd be paying more than double what the whole fence was really worth to his mate, while he only had to give his mate a carton of beer. My dad dropped his voice down to a strong and firm tone and listed their options under law and what he intended to do. The neighbour then stormed off and called the police, who came out to investigate allegations of verbal abuse, which didn't get anywhere near court because my dad could produce reputable character witnesses from all over town who said they've never heard him raise his voice or swear during an argument in his entire life. In fact, he always does the complete opposite – drop his tone to a very commanding Darth Vader-type voice to state his case and advise his opponent of what they have to do if they want to get anywhere with him.

Student challenge 15: Tax scales for your pay packet, page 166

Assuming you are an Australian citizen but don't have any tax deductions for donations to charities or work expenses (for compulsory uniforms etc) use the PAYG (Pay As You Go) tax scales on page 166 to work out how much tax you'd pay per year if your total annual income is:

a. $5000 . . . answer =   no tax for the year
b. $25,000 . . . answer = [(25,000 – 21,600) × 0.30] = $3672
c. $65,000 . . . answer = [2652 + 9119 + 4409 + {(65,000 – 62501) ×.47}] = $17, 355

THE SOLUTION TO KIRBY'S STICK PUZZLE (PAGE 203)

Kirby rotated the minus sign 90 degrees as she shifted it to the front and the roman numeral ten automatically turned into a multiplication sign, like this:

$$I \times I = I$$

Moral of the story: Sometimes the simplest solutions are hiding right in front of your face.

Now use this story to help discuss Rules 6 and 29 of Success with your child (see page 227).

Additional exercise: Did Kirby trick you too? Now see if you can make a deal with your parents/children to double pocket money for the week if they can't/can solve it! (Of course double nothing is still nothing, so if your family doesn't operate with weekly pocket money, maybe you'll have to negotiate some extra chores around the house!)

SOLUTION TO KIRBY'S CHAT ROOM PUZZLE (SEE PAGE 205)

Kirby added a line to turn the number ten into the word 'to' so the puzzle changed from a math's problem into the time of day.
Like this:

$$20 \text{ TO } 5 = 4.40$$

Moral of the story: Sometimes it only takes one small idea to find big solutions in a different direction.

Now use this story to help discuss Rules 29 and 33 of Success with your child (see page 227).

Appendix II

50 Fun Rules for Success

Throughout this book and the novels in the *Kirby's Crusader* series (for ages eight to 15) you'll see mention of my 50 Fun Rules for Success, most of which I had to learn the hard way, just as the fictional characters do in each of my children's stories. They're a combination of universal truths, popular maxims and lessons that I collected in my diaries over the years to help me stay motivated and see the bright side of bad luck whenever it struck me. So you may have heard some of these from time to time or else learned them the hard way too. Here they are in one place, so that hopefully, the next generation may find them equally amusing and helpful.

1. Protect your ass(ets) – enemies can be anywhere.
2. If you can't earn it, learn it.
3. Smart kids smell profit in the wind.
4. Quick cash is loathe to last.
5. A buck saved by shopping around is as good as a buck and a half of labour.
6. Defeat your corporate enemy with strategy, not fighting.
7. Exploit your strengths and your competitor's weaknesses.
8. Goods are as good as money.
9. Skills are the foundation of wealth.
10. Knowledge is power but generosity is freedom and honour is forever.

11. The bigger the promise of return on your investment, the bigger the risk.

12. Never put all your financial eggs in one basket.

13. Making a living is not the same as making a life.
    OR You work to live, not live to work. But find a job you enjoy and you're partying all the time.

14. There's no shame in being poor, only in behaving poorly.

15. An overdue chore? Do it now, do it now, do it now!

16. All things in order of priority.

17. Clients forget what you said and what you did, but never how you make them feel.

18. Every job has a downside, so do the crap first and get on with the good part.

19. The boss/client with the biggest mouth usually has an equally large aperture at the other end.

20. Want to know how long you'll be missed after you leave your job? Stick your hand in a bucket of water, shake it up, remove your hand and time how long the ripples take to settle.

21. Good luck is the shadow of good people.

22. A business person without morals is a criminal.

23. You don't have to be greedy to be wealthy.

24. It only takes one step to keep ahead of the pack.

25. Say yes to opportunity and figure out how to cope later.

26. Embrace change as a challenge, don't fear it.

27. In chaos, lurks opportunity.

28. Just because you serve someone, doesn't make you their servant.

29. Sometimes the simplest solutions are hiding right in front of your face.

30. Judge wealth by the generosity of the heart, not the size of their wallet.

31. Beware the businessperson whose flashy car is also their office, their advertisement and their bedroom.

32. It takes two years to learn how to talk and the rest of your life to figure out when to shut up.

33. If you take the wrong path, back up and try again with a different direction.

34. If you're falling, you might as well flap your arms and try the impossible.

35. If you're pushed, push back hardest when they're not looking.

36. Aim for the moon, and then if you miss, at least you'll still land amongst the stars.

    OR If you aim for mediocrity, it's all you're likely to achieve.

37. Great rewards wait for they who brave the hardest path.

38. Success without effort is empty.

39. Success without honesty is a vacuum. It sucks everyone in.

40. Every workplace has someone who'll betray you, someone who'll support you and someone who only shows up to get their pay cheque.

41. The fastest way to get stabbed in the back is to let strangers behind you.

42. Never do business with friends, family or ex-boyfriends/girlfriends.

43.   Some people are meant to be leaders, most of us are content to be led, and the rest are couch-sitters with mouths gaping, waiting to be fed.

44.   Failing to plan = planning to fail.

45.   Never swear at a nasty customer. There are much more creative ways to have fun with them.

46.   If you don't make it happen, who will?

47.   If you don't care about yourself, how can you expect or deserve anyone else to?

48.   Don't be the traveller who takes every shortcut and misses the adventure.

49.   Competitors are good for business.

50.   Niche marketing is good for business. (No competitors!)

Here's space to add your own favourite words of wisdom for your children:

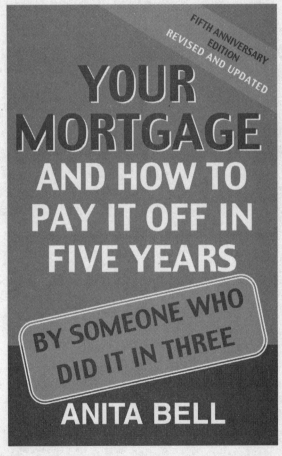

Your Money: Starting out and starting over
For ages 16 to adult, this book helps you get and keep a clean
financial slate and includes my favourite top 10 easy steps for
investing in the share market.

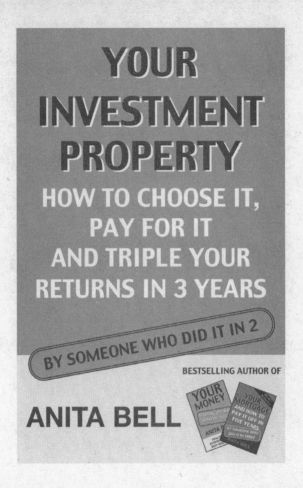

Your Investment Property: How to choose it, pay for it and triple your returns in three years
A must for anyone planning to invest in property. This book is packed with helpful tips and shortcuts to use and adapt, regardless of which investment strategy you're using.

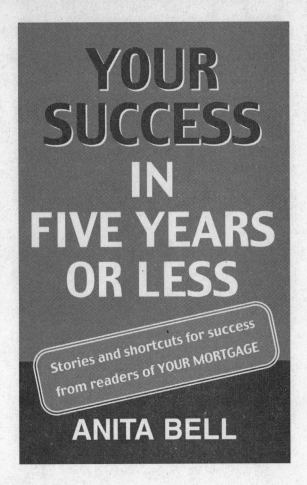

YOUR SUCCESS IN FIVE YEARS OR LESS

Stories and shortcuts for success from readers of YOUR MORTGAGE

ANITA BELL

Your Success in Five Years or Less
Provides a cross-section of real-life case studies from readers of
the *Your Mortgage* series who've adapted tips to suit their own
Aussie-battler circumstances and saved many thousands of
dollars each. Also provides a crash course with tips and shortcuts to help you catch up.

Your Real Estate Jargon Explained and *Your Sharemarket Jargon Explained*

Two pocket-sized beginner-guides for ages 14 to adult. In addition to the definitions, each booklet is packed with fun tips, warnings and shortcuts. Together they provide a snapshot for both sides of an investor's proverbial 'flipped coin' when trying to decide whether to sink money into property or the sharemarket.

Finance-related fiction
(Soft financial concepts for ages 8 to 13)

Note: Kirby's Crusaders is an action-packed thriller series for kids, which mixes fun and finance with each title in the series featuring two of the 50 Fun Rules for Success.

Kirby's Crusaders 1: Tagged by Dead Dogs
A group of fictional teenagers earn half a million dollars fighting true-crime. Winner of the 2003 International Crime Stoppers Award (print media).

Kirby's Crusaders 2: Hunt the Hunters
The teen crusaders set up a company, purchase assets and fight
a hostile corporate attack.

Kirby's Crusaders 3: Coming soon . . .